Catskill Trails: A Ranger's Guide to the High Peaks, Book One, The Northern Catskills

The author paints verbal pictures of the region not often found in guidebooks. ... The chapter on Bearpen is exceptional, making me want to put my boots on and get there as soon as possible.

Trailwalker

A valuable guide for both novice and seasoned hikers.

Kaatskill Life

Catskill Trails: A Ranger's Guide to the High Peaks, Book Two, The Central Catskills

A must. ... The small paperback is the perfect size for on-the-trail reference and its format, in which point-to-point directions are separated from the superbly written trail descriptions, makes it a delight for armchair hikers as well.

Hudson Valley Magazine

Edward Henry gives us more than a guide to the trails and peaks of the Catskills; he lets us vicariously experience a hike, the real hike of a natural historian, and teaches us to see more than a dirt path, green trees, and craggy hills.

New York History

If you prepare for hikes by reading about them, or want the accumulated knowledge of a veteran forest ranger while traipsing through the woods, Henry will satisfy you.

Trailwalker

As you prepare for this season's Catskill hiking, I would add an eleventh to Edward Henry's ten Hiking Rules and Guidelines: pack and use Catskill Trails.

New York State Conservationist

Gunks Trails: A Ranger's Guide to the Shawangunk Mountains

Occasionally ... a book comes our way that is different from our usual fare, yet so excellent that we would be remiss not to draw your attention to it. Gunks Trails *is such a book.*

New York History

Each hike becomes a lesson in ecology and history. ... This is an excellent guide for the first-time Gunks visitor, and has some interesting tidbits for the seasoned Gunks traveler as well.

New York State Conservationist

Henry writes like a photographer sees.

Catskill Mountain Region Guide

Henry ... is a fine nature writer who even manages to make sense of the confusing geology of the Gunks.

Hudson Valley Magazine

... what distinguishes this guide is the knowledge and perspective Henry has gained as a park ranger and employee of the U.S. Forest Service. ... The tidy publication is packed with the kind of detailed information that makes it worth taking along to review while visiting the site.

River Reporter, Literary Gazette

Berkshire & Taconic Trails
A Ranger's Guide

Published by

Black Dome Press Corp.
PO Box 64, Catskill, NY 12414
www.blackdomepress.com   518-577-5238

First Edition Paperback 2008

Library of Congress Cataloging-in-Publication Data

Henry, Edward G.
  Berkshire & Taconic trails : a ranger's guide / Edward G. Henry. — 1st ed.
     p. cm.
  Includes bibliographical references and index.
  ISBN 978-1-883789-56-5 (pbk.)
 1. Hiking--Massachusetts—Berkshire Hills—Guidebooks. 2. Trails—Massachusetts—Berkshire Hills—Guidebooks. 3. Hiking—Massachusetts—Taconic Trail System—Guidebooks. 4. Trails—Massachusetts—Taconic Range—Guidebooks. 5. Berkshire Hills (Mass.)—Guidebooks. 6. Taconic Trail System (Mass.)—Guidebooks. I. Title.

 GV199.42.M42B4733 2008
 917.44'10444--dc22

2007045807

Outdoor recreational activities are by their very nature potentially hazardous and contain risk. See "Caution" page xiv.

All photographs by Edward G. Henry

Cover: Mount Greylock

Frontispiece: Looking West from Monument Mountain

Design: Toelke Associates

Maps created with TOPO! software © 2006 National Geographic Maps. To learn more visit: http://www.nationalgeographic.com/topo

Printed in the USA

10 9 8 7 6 5 4 3 2

Berkshire & Taconic TRAILS

Edward G. Henry

BLACK·DOME

For Alex

When people ask me which hike is my favorite,
the answer is the last hike I took with you.

CONTENTS

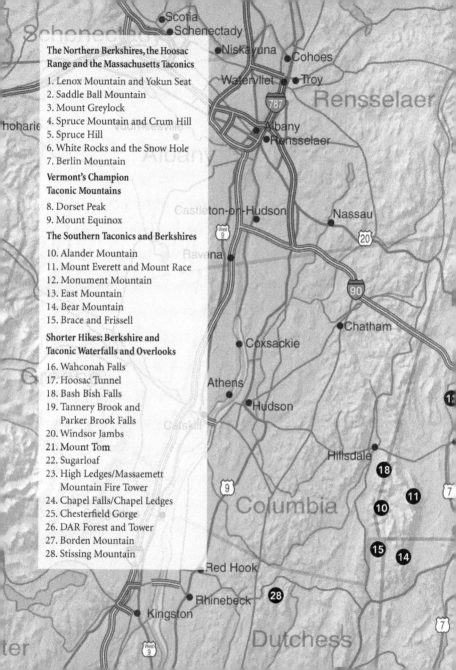

ACKNOWLEDGMENTS

Like the numerous hills and mountains that, together, make up the Taconics and the Berkshires, there are so many people that helped in making this book that I cannot possibly name them all. Still, there are some that rise so prominently that they deserve special mention. First, my gratitude goes out to Shawn Keizer and John Butnor—two of my lifelong friends that lift me and my efforts to the greatest of heights. Both of these friends visited and explored many of the places in this book with me and, in some ways, when you read these pages, you are hiking with Shawn and John as well.

I cannot say enough about my publisher, Deborah Allen, and I am pleased to call her a friend as well. Through the years, Deborah and her husband, Bob Hoch, have been great to me and my family and I appreciate it more than they know. They are the most pleasant of people to work with, and to spend time with as well. Steve Hoare, my editor, is always great to work with and a top-notch editor to boot.

I also want to thank all those people who helped with the editorial aspects of this book, especially Mike Olexa, Kim Halpin, Matina Billias and Natalie Mortensen. I want to thank Congressman John Olver for taking the time to share some of his thoughts and passion for the Taconics and the Berkshires by writing this book's foreword. Then, there is the supporting cast who has been my foundation throughout this effort and throughout my life in general. First and foremost are my parents, sister and extended family. I also want to mention my friends and coworkers at the Wallkill River National Wildlife Refuge, including Bill Koch, Jamie Britt, Dan Stotts, Mike Durfee, Fran Stevenson, Marie Springer, Laura Mitchell, Blair Mace and Rick Volick.

In addition I want to thank Bill Kuhne, Reggie Carlson, Rob Overton, Debbie Willis, and Jeff Underwood.

And, of course, the last six years of my life would never have been as rich and fulfilling as they were without my daughter Alexandria Bui-Henry, my pride and joy. I look forward to exploring our world as we grow together. It is all the great people in my life that have made me what I am and, in turn, made this book what it is.

CAUTION

Outdoor recreational activities are by their very nature potentially hazardous and contain risk. All participants in such activities must assume the responsibility for their own actions and safety. No book can replace good judgment. The outdoors is forever changing. The author and publisher cannot be held responsible for inaccuracies, errors, or omissions, or for any changes in the details of this publication, or for the consequences of any reliance on the information contained herein, or for the safety of people in the outdoors.

Hiking Rules and Guidelines

1. Dress appropriately for the season and trail—cotton retains water and leads to body heat loss. Wear sturdy shoes. Hypothermia and foot injuries are the leading causes of emergency evacuations. Wear proper sun protection—hat, sunglasses, sunscreen—appropriate to the season. Wear and use appropriate snow gear when the trails are snow-covered.

2. Be prepared: have a first-aid kit, whistle, flashlight, matches, emergency blanket, extra high-energy food, and water (at least 24 ounces per person). Do not drink untreated water from streams.

3. Do not use or create shortcuts. These can be dangerous and encourage erosion.

4. Respect private property rights. Do not trespass. Get permission before entering private land.

5. Camp only in designated areas. Regulations vary in the four states and among the various land managers in the Taconics and Berkshires.

And remember: if you carry it in, carry it out!

Foreword

Tucked in between the Green Mountains to the north and the Catskills to the west, and with various population centers in all directions, the Berkshire/Taconic range has long been a destination for tourists seeking haven from the hustle and bustle of outlying urban areas. Once isolated and hardly reachable, it took the late arrival of the locomotive (via the Hoosac Tunnel) and the eventual opening of major routes like the Mohawk Trail to open up this land of lush habitats and diverse forest to a population now firmly entrenched in its own unique settlements and cultural history.

As Edward G. Henry explains in the following pages, it is an area originally formed by the impact of the ice age upon metamorphic rock of complex layering and mineralogy, and to this day the Taconic Mountains display the moraines, drumlins and exposed glacial features that were left behind. And nothing is better than a good hike to reach an understanding of this unique geological setting. What better than a first-hand experience with the mountaintops, waterfalls, valleys and forests that have formed a welcome retreat for so many people?

As an avid user of our natural settings myself, I can personally testify to the grandeur of the Taconics and the Berkshires. I have walked the Appalachian Trail through the Berkshires, and climbed the rocks of the Shawangunk Mountains. And I am proud to have been part of such initiatives as the Housatonic River Valley Heritage Area, the Ashuwillticook Bike Path, and the preservation of 1,000 acres of protected forest at Camp Hi-Rock in Mt. Washington, a diverse swath of forest whose beauty is at the essence of the Berkshire Taconic Range.

Some natives say there's a special spirit that emanates from the hills and valleys, and that the land and its rivers form an inseparable part of themselves. And that this spirit has been noted down through the ages, back to the days when the Mahicans held council, a tribe whose name I've heard translated magnificently as "the people-of-the-continually-flowing-waters."

From geological insights to geographical oversights, Edward G. Henry provides a detailed portrayal of the Berkshires and other-named mountain ranges that form part and parcel of the Taconic Mountain Range. (We learn, for example, that the Taconic "giants," Mount Greylock and Mount Everett, are erroneously associated with the Berkshires.) His guide takes you not only to the place, but to the moment, and enhances one's appreciation of the land, rivers, forests and vistas that make up this remarkable place.

John W. Olver
Member of Congress
Amherst, Massachusetts

INTRODUCTION
The Taconics and the Berkshires

Overview

The Taconic Mountains form a thin high line along New England's western edge. Rolling hills and low mountains fill western New England and the eastern side of New York's Hudson Valley. Scenic highways and byways crisscross the region. Millions upon millions of people drive though the region admiring the scenery, but few stop to explore. Stretching through most of Dutchess, Columbia and Rensselaer counties in New York State, the Taconics even make a small appearance on the Hudson River's western flank as the 725-foot Cronomer Hill in Newburgh. While New York is a constant host to the mountains' western flank, the Taconics' eastern edge runs from northwestern Connecticut to southwestern Vermont. The mountains generally increase in elevation as they head north, with a notable exception at the 2,602-foot Mount Everett in southern Massachusetts.

While the Taconics comprise the region's dominant geological background and physical geography, it is "The Berkshires" that are world-renowned as a summer retreat and cultural center. In the 1800s, when the railroad was king, the Berkshires—particularly the area between Great Barrington and Lenox, Massachusetts—were summer playgrounds for the rich and famous. Only a few active remnants of this heritage remain, but the area's natural beauty still compares with the Northeast's higher, better-known mountain ranges. Many "Berkshire" landmarks are actually Taconic landforms, yet to most of the world, the Taconics remain obscure. Tanglewood, Williams College, Bash Bish and Mount Greylock are all names associated with the Berkshires that are, in fact, Taconic sites.

Almost everyone familiar with New York and New England has traveled through the area on Interstates 90 and 84 or on the Taconic

Parkway, the first four-lane limited-access highway in America. The region's beauty is apparent even from these major transportation arteries, but the Berkshires' and Taconics' true beauty merely begins at these highways. Amazing views from Mount Greylock and Race Mountain, the lacy beauty of Bash Bish Falls and Chesterfield Gorge, and the curiosities of the Snow Hole and Bear Mountain provide ample reasons to exit the area's major transportation arteries and explore.

Geology and Geography

The majority of the Taconic Mountains straddle the Connecticut, New York, Massachusetts, and Vermont borders for more than 150 miles. Unlike many mountain-defined boundaries that follow a range's highest ridge, these straight state borders slice the landscape without regard for natural features. One result of this decision is a loss of continuity for the Taconics as a mountain range in the eyes of people and governments. When looking at a map of any one of these states, the impression made by the Taconics is much diminished compared to the range seen as a whole.

Typically, the disciplines of geography and geology overlap, especially when referring to regional landscapes. The Taconics and the Berkshires, however, are an exception and a hard area to define. Although not perfectly outlined, the Berkshire rocks and their associated hills fill western Massachusetts from the Taconic and Hoosac mountains to the Connecticut Valley. The main reason for this is a blending of mountainous zones, which are more geological cousins than a single unit. Unfortunately, few organizations, public or private, treat the Taconic Mountains as a continuous body. In Massachusetts, people and organizations blend the Taconics with the smaller Hoosac Range and the expansive Berkshire Hills. As a result, understanding the region's geology and natural history is difficult.

The Berkshires rise as a series of complex bedrock skeletons that uphold a swath of hills and mountains running between the Connecticut Valley and the Housatonic Valley. Much older than the Hoosac and Taconic formations, Berkshire rocks are deformed members of the billion-year-old Grenville province, which forms North America's core. During early mountain-building events, magma worked its way into these Grenville rocks. Today, these harder, erosion-resistant granites and their metamorphic kin form many Berkshire summits. Line after line of rounded, erosion-resistant 1,800 to 2,100-foot hills fill this region. Only the slender, deep valleys of the Westfield and Deerfield rivers and their tributaries dissect this rugged land. In addition, a few of the prominent points along the Connecticut River, such as Sugarloaf Mountain and the Holyoke Range, are sometimes added to this prestigious range of hills, but these areas have a distinct geology.

In contrast with the Berkshires, the Taconics are displaced remnants of massive thrust faulting. Taconic rocks were propelled westward over the Berkshire and Green mountain strata. The rock came to rest on limestones and dolomites that formed around the same time as the Taconic strata. Both the Taconic and Berkshire strata are highly tilted—perpendicular, rather than parallel to their original positions— so most of the exposed rock layers are observed in cross section.

The Taconics are a significant mountain range and an integral component of the Appalachian Mountains. Topping out at 3,848 feet on Vermont's Mount Equinox, the Taconics provide the 97th and 99th (3,770-foot Dorset Peak) highest peaks in New England. In Massachusetts, the Taconics climb to 3,491 feet on Mount Greylock, the Bay State's highest point. No other mountain in Massachusetts off the Mount Greylock elevational island even attains 3,000 feet. In New York, the Taconics support 2,818-foot Berlin Mountain, the highest point in the state not in the Adirondacks or in the Catskills. In Connecticut, the Taconics uphold the two highest points in the state, a shoulder of Mount Frissell, at 2,380 feet, and the state's highest peak, 2,316-foot Bear Mountain.

Geologically, this confusion adds to the lack of identity the Taconic Mountains receive. All too often, 2,602-foot Mount Everett, a distinctly Taconic peak and a mountain soaring well above its neighbors, is described as a Berkshire peak. Mount Greylock, the highest point in Massachusetts, is a Taconic giant, but again is often associated with the Berkshires. And while the Taconics and the Berkshires clearly overlap in Massachusetts, and to a lesser extent in New York and Connecticut, the term "Berkshire" is practically a foreign language in Vermont. In the Green Mountain State, the Taconics extend north for nearly fifty miles to Rutland, with numerous peaks topping 3,000 feet.

When it comes to geology and scenery, the Taconics can be summed up in a single word: windows. It is not often that one word captures the essence of a place, yet among the rolling hills and low mountains of the Taconics and Berkshires, "windows" clearly creates an accurate picture of this inviting landscape. As a mountain range, the Taconic Mountains are a transplanted and disfigured set of rocks. Thrust atop other layers in a series of earthquakes that rocked the North American continent, the present-day mountains lie atop limestone layers. In places, the hard Taconic rocks have worn away, leaving windows into the limestone valleys. A perfect example of this lies just west of Mount Everett. A sheet of upthrusted Everett schists eroded away to expose the Walloomsac limy muds that compose much of the isolated Guilder Brook watershed. So, whether it is a description of the exposed limestones and dolomites or the countless picture-perfect scenes framed by the region's many viewpoints, the word "window" is quintessential in describing the Taconics and the Berkshires.

The Taconics are a geologic island. Isolated in geological time and rock type from the surrounding area and even from their own basement rock, the Taconic Mountains stand alone. During the Taconic

Mountain-building event, an island arc resembling Japan plowed into North America, and a huge mountain chain arose along the continent's east coast. At the same time, a massive quantity of older rock lying against what would become raw material for the Green Mountains was literally pushed onto its side and over the rock to its west. At least 150 miles long and from 5 to 30 miles across, the sheared material was placed on top of younger limestones and other calcareous Ordovician rocks. More resistant to erosion, this isolated rock mass has persisted in its new location, and when North America's eastern fringe rose again, it created the Taconic Mountains.

Formed of a wide range of metamorphic rocks, the Taconics display complex sets of mineralogy and layering. The gradation of the metamorphic rocks from the relatively low-grade phylites and slates into high-grade schists and gneisses over the course of a few miles seems to defy the rules of metamorphic formation. An explanation lies in the massive tilting and faulting that upended and stacked these rock layers that formed dozens of miles from one another. Stacked like a deck of cards haphazardly pushed onto its side, the current orientation of the Taconics' rocks is very different from their original positions. The farther east the original slice, the farther it had to move. As a result, the first slices that pushed west—such as the Everett schists—contain no gneisses, but the Berkshire peaks to the east have significant amounts of gneiss formed from North America's deep roots. Along the mountains' edges, the slate belt of Vermont and New York—lower-grade metamorphic products—provides a valuable building material.

The recent ice age completely covered the Taconics and the Berkshires. Each time the ice advanced, the mountains received an additional erosional treatment. In four separate advances—the Kansan, Nebraskan, Illinoisian and Wisconsin—mile-thick ice sheets buried the valleys and covered the mountaintops. The grinding, scraping ice softened corners and steepened slopes, turning a V-shaped mountain range into a U-shaped landscape. Upon retreating, the ice left masses of till up to 200 feet thick in the valleys and lesser amounts in the higher elevations. In some places knobs of Taconic phyllite and graywackes protrude from this till-filled landscape. Unlike many adjoining areas, few distinct moraines reveal the glaciers' retreat. Within the Taconics and the Berkshires, ice dams created huge, but ephemeral, glacial lakes that rivaled their descendants such as Lake Champlain and the Great Lakes. Fine soils and organic mucks accumulated on the lake bottoms, and when combined with the ubiquitous glacial tills, the former lake beds provide prime agricultural land.

Although not a dominant part of the landscape, drumlins are a significant glacial feature found throughout the region. These drumlins and associated glacial striations reveal that the last glacial advance came from the northwest, out of New York. Glacial striations are scratches made by hard rocks that are trapped in the advancing glacier; they scrape and scour the softer bedrock. The last ice sheet to cover the area, the Hudson-Champlain lobe, advanced as far south as Long Island, where it deposited its terminal moraine on the island.

Additional curiosities fill the Taconic region. "Boulder trains" are one example. Massive rocks plucked from The Knob lie scattered in two lines for about twenty miles to the south and southeast of this 1,600-foot hill. Named the Richland Boulder Train, the scattered amphibole boulders are a distinct geological feature. A second, smaller boulder train, the Great Barrington Train, may also have originated from The Knob, but the origin of these highly weathered rocks is debated. The Knob rises just north of Queechy Lake, its steep eastern face paralleling New York State's Route 22 between New Lebanon and Queechy.

Rivers

The Taconics are drained by many rivers, but the Housatonic, more so than any other, may be claimed by the Taconics as its own. Rising from the slopes of Mount Greylock and the neighboring Berkshires to the east, the river flows through Pittsfield and then into the southern Taconics and the Litchfield Hills, Connecticut's name for the Taconics. Named by the Mahican Indians for its meaning of "beyond the mountain place," the *Wussi-adene-uk* slowly evolved into the modern "Housatonic." In the mid-1800s, artists from the Hudson River School of painting featured the river and surrounding mountains on many canvases. Sadly, this "beyond the mountain place" was the recipient of tons and tons of PCBs from industrial activity in the Pittsfield area. Instead of a legacy of trout and mountain fishing, the river's course must endure a tangle of environmental legal battles and a cleanup rivaling that along the Hudson. Once completing its southeasterly journey through Connecticut, the river flows into the Long Island Sound at Bridgeport.

The Hoosic River, a tributary of the Hudson, is also almost exclusively a Taconic and a Berkshire river. Its waters arise north of the Pittsfield area and drain Adams, North Adams and Williamstown before cutting through the southwestern-most corner of Vermont, crossing into Rensselaer County in New York and draining into the Hudson. Constrained within a narrow valley, the river provided a great deal of waterpower for nineteenth-century industries such as paper, textile and food production. At the same time, the valley subjected the area to a number of devastating floods. Many of the towns along the river channeled the river in an attempt to alleviate the flooding. As a result, the river often flows through concrete canyons.

In the Berkshires, two tributaries of the Connecticut River, the Westfield and Deerfield, drain the mountainous terrain. Both cut through a variety of pastoral valleys and deep gorges, and host a large number of sprightly tributaries steeped in small waterfalls and cascades. The Deerfield River, in both Massachusetts and then heading into Vermont's Green Mountains, offers great auto-touring routes, especially in fall.

When exploring the region, the overall feel of the peaceful green mountains, soothing waterfalls and splendid valleys is easy to experience, but hard to describe. Full of inspiring landscapes and hidden gems, the region's landscape is among the least appreciated in the Appalachians. Mount Equinox in Vermont, Mount Greylock in Massachusetts, Berlin Mountain in New York and Bear Mountain in Connecticut provide the region's highest points and unveil landscapes more varied than their common geology would suggest. Attempting to describe the Taconics and the Berkshires is similar to hiking a mountain without a marked trail: the task becomes jumbled and confusing even before it is begun.

History

Despite the geological and geographical oversights and mischaracterizations so prominent within the region, the area does have a shared settlement and cultural history. With its main access from the Housatonic and Hoosic river valleys, it is not surprising that more settlers entered this region from Connecticut and New York than from eastern Massachusetts. As a result, that distinctive Boston accent is absent from the region's communities, and most of the early transportation links were with the south and west.

In fact, penetrating this unyielding expanse of steep hills, valleys and, in some cases, mountain walls, is the stuff of transportation legend. Among the most important, but underappreciated, efforts of the Revolutionary War was the 1775–76 journey taken by Colonel (later General) Henry Knox, who transported fifty-nine guns from Fort Ticonderoga to Boston—a journey of more than 300 miles that took almost two months to complete. The army used specially constructed sleds to slide the guns over the snow and ice. Their chosen route generally traversed the Taconics and the Berkshires along what is now Route 23 in eastern New York and western Massachusetts. Along the route were the towns of Hillsdale, Egremont and Great Barrington. Without these heavy armaments, the colonial attempt to rid Boston of the British may have never succeeded.

In the 1800s the region's transportation challenge turned to the railroad. When mentioned together, railroads and the Berkshires can only mean one thing: the Hoosac Tunnel. This five-mile tunnel, built at a huge expense in money, time and lives, eventually solved the challenge of providing a direct link from Boston to the west side of the Berkshires. Even with the Industrial Revolution and its huge impact on the Northeast, this important transportation link was not completed until 1878. Railroads stretched from coast to coast long before rails crossed the Berkshires.

Roads also took a long time to be built through the region. Hard metamorphic rocks and steep narrow valleys made road-building difficult and expensive. All of the routes have impressive climbs and drops as they cross the Berkshires and, in most cases, the Taconics as well. U.S. Route 20, also known as Jacob's Ladder, follows the Westfield River before ascending hard layers of gneiss and topping the Berkshires. West of Pittsfield the highway crosses the Taconics' main ridge at just above 1,500 feet. From the Connecticut Valley, State Route 9 follows the Mill River drainage into Goshen, where it picks up the Swift River and then Westfield River before climbing to 2,040 feet at the top of the Berkshires in Windsor. Then the route rapidly descends into Dalton and Pittsfield, where it ends. The scenic and famous Mohawk Trail, State Route 2, runs from Greenfield along the Deerfield River before crossing over the Hoosac Range at 2,180 feet and then plunging into the Hoosic Valley at North Adams. Route 2 then heads over the 2,100-foot Petersburg Pass.

Only the Mass Pike, Interstate 90, offers a speedy passage through the Taconics and the Berkshires. The superhighway's route pretty much ignores the terrain's challenges. A sign between mile markers 19 and 20 identifies the highest point on Route 90 east of Ocoma, South Dakota, a town just west of the Missouri River.

Along with agriculture, iron ore from the southern part of the range helped support first the American Revolution and then the nation's first industries. The iron ore was among the highest quality in the world. Bog iron was mixed with limestone and processed with charcoal, giving rise to fledgling industries and to the first removal of the region's primordial forests. Limestone for building came from quarries in Connecticut, Massachusetts and Vermont. Paper mills flourished as well, especially along the upper Housatonic Valley. Crane Paper, a company that produced paper for U.S. currency, started in Dalton in the early nineteenth century. By the 1840s the region produced more than 20 percent of the nation's paper.

In the mid and late 1800s, tourists, especially wealthy families from New York City, would come to the Berkshires. Along with Newport, Rhode Island, towns like Great Barrington, Lenox and Stockbridge were among the greatest places to escape summer's heat. Artists and writers flocked to the area. William Cullen Bryant transformed his law career into that of a writer and artist while in Great Barrington. Herman Melville often retreated to the Berkshires' hills and valleys to ponder nature's wonder. Although many of the destinations were physically part of the Taconic Mountains, the name "Berkshire" became the region's dominant identifier. Grand hotels and resorts lined the region's rivers from the Housatonic to the Connecticut.

In the nineteenth century, art and wilderness combined to foster North America's first artistic style—the Hudson River School of landscape painting. The artists of the Hudson River School were no strangers to the Taconics or to the Berkshires. Thomas Cole, the school's founder and one of its most renowned artists, painted *View of Hoosac Mountain and Pontoosuc Lake near Pittsfield, Massachusetts.* The painting reveals the uneasy mix of pastoral valleys and rugged wilderness that covered much of the then-fledgling United States. Asher B. Durand, Frederic Church, John Kensett, and George Inness were among other notable painters to study and paint in the region. Monument Mountain, the Holyoke Range, the Stockbridge Bowl and Hoosac Mountain (Mount Greylock) all graced Hudson River School canvases.

Climate and Wildlife

One of the most diverse aspects of the Taconics and the Berkshires is its climate. Stretching from Rutland, Vermont, down almost to Danbury, Connecticut, these mountains vary greatly in both temperature and precipitation. In addition, the variation in elevation of up to 3,000 feet adds to the differences in precipitation and temperature.

The result of this great variability in climate is a lot of freezing and thawing and a constant promise of changing weather conditions. Rocks erode faster under such conditions, but these mountains' natural resistance moderates the breakdown. Vegetation, too, must deal with the variation and be able to withstand bitter cold and blazing heat, floods and droughts.

Wildlife as well must adapt to the diverse conditions. Many migratory birds use the area for a summer nesting ground. With large stretches of unbroken forest, many forest-interior species can thrive. Raptors, including hawks, falcons, and the occasional eagle, also do well in the region. Game birds such as turkey and grouse roam the woods. Mammals thrive in the Taconics, with sightings of skunks, raccoons, deer, foxes, coyotes and bears being common.

In addition to the hikes in this book, the Berkshires and the Taconics offer many other places worth exploring that can add to the understanding of their geological setting. Either because the hike is too short, the drive is too long for the trip to be worthwhile, or the surroundings are too developed, the overall experience of these places does not reach the level of the hikes chosen for this book. Still, it would be unfair not to mention places such as Cronomer Hill in Newburgh, New York, The Dome in southern Vermont, Kent Falls and the Lions Head in northwestern Connecticut, Natural Bridge in North Adams, and October and Tekoa mountains in the Berkshires.

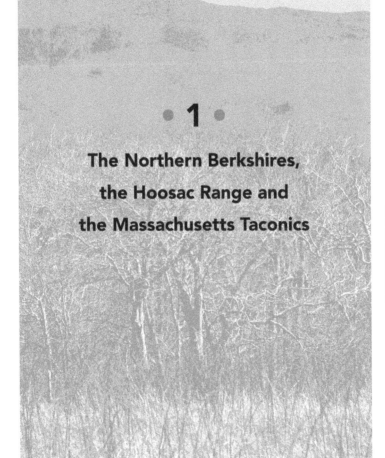

• 1 •

The Northern Berkshires,
the Hoosac Range and
the Massachusetts Taconics

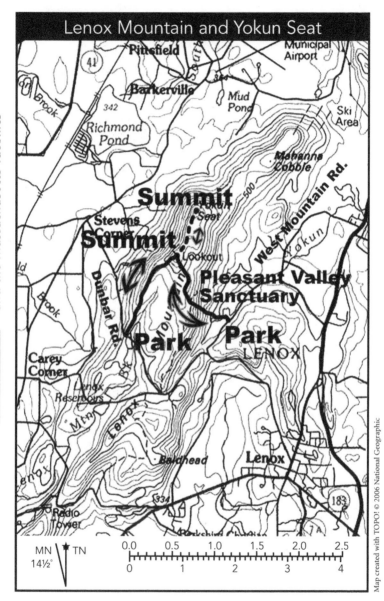

The Northern Berkshires, the Hoosac Range and the Massachusetts Taconics

Map created with TOPO! © 2006 National Geographic

Lenox Mountain and Yokun Seat

Highlights: Bird watching; View from Yokun Seat

Option 1, via Pleasant Valley Wildlife Sanctuary

Hike Length: 3.7 miles round trip
Hike Difficulty: Moderate
Starting Elevation: 1370'
Highest Elevation: 2150'

Option 2 (Dunbar Road)

Hike Length: 3.6 miles round trip
Hike Difficulty: Easy to moderate
Starting Elevation: 1645'
Highest Elevation: 2150'

Directions:

Option 1, via Pleasant Valley Wildlife Sanctuary:
US 7/20 to W. Dugway Rd. (.6 miles north of 7/20 split).
Go west on W. Dugway Rd. for .8 miles to W. Mountain
Rd. Turn left onto W. Mountain Rd. Continue to Pleasant
Valley Sanctuary, .8 miles on right.

Option 2, via Dunbar Rd.:
From MA 7A (Main St. in Lenox) take Cliftwood St. (west)
.8 miles to Reservoir Rd. Take Reservoir Rd. for about 1.5
miles (pass split with W. Mountain Rd. on right). Take right
on Dunbar Rd., and go .8 miles to parking area.

GPS:

Parking (Dunbar Rd.):	42°22.81; 73°19.36
Parking (Pleasant Valley):	42°22.95; 73°17.91
Lenox Summit:	42°23.59; 73°18.65
Yokun Seat:	42°24.05; 73°18.39

Like many Taconic destinations, Lenox Mountain and Yokun Seat have more than one good approach. Season, challenge, day of the week, and parking fees all can factor into choosing the route to Lenox Mountain's top ridge. Once reaching the summit, with its weary fire tower and view sliced and diced by fences, wire and wood, disappointment is inevitable. From there, however, begins the route to the mountain's true treasure, Yokun Seat, which lies farther north along the same ridgeline. Like much of the Berkshires, true isolation is hard to find on Lenox Mountain, yet the amazing scenery and great views offer a compelling hike.

Via the Pleasant Valley Wildlife Sanctuary

The Pleasant Valley Wildlife Sanctuary is a 1,300-acre preserve that sits atop calcium-rich soils and provides an extraordinary lushness and diversity. Pleasant Valley and the lower reaches of Yokun Creek host beaver ponds and an impressive display of flowers, both wild and planted. Managed by the Massachusetts Audubon Society, there is a fee for accessing the area, and the site is closed on many Mondays. The beauty of the well-groomed trails and waterways and the knowledge offered in the nature center is a double-edged sword when it comes to finding solitude in the mountains. Still, once on the mountain slopes, the less-visited terrain offers a quiet and serene hike.

The well-maintained, attractive trail to ascend Lenox Mountain begins at the nature center and then heads past Pike's Pond, a great setting for relaxation and bird watching. Trails follow both sides of Pike's Pond, and both routes meet again before the Trail of the Ledges heads up the mountain. Throughout the preserve, blue-marked trails indicate a trail moving away from the main office, while yellow-marked trails head toward it. The mowed paths cut through open fields, and well-maintained dirt trails pass through the forest. Along some of the wetlands, boardwalks provide easy walking. A great number of animals live among the lush habitats, their sounds even more prevalent than their sightings. Great egrets, tree swallows, songbirds, frogs and even fish are hard not to notice. Through it all is the gentle tumble of water. Surrounding the open areas is a healthy and diverse second-growth forest of basswood, sugar maple, northern red oak, American beech, yellow birch, and white ash. The trees grow straight and tall, topping out at seventy feet. White pine crowns rise above this healthy forest. Rich soils helped the regrowth attain its great diversity and lushness. Along the forest edge, where light is more plentiful, a thick understory of saplings, shrubs, ferns and wildflowers abounds.

As the softer marbles lining the ponds and valleys give way to the building mountain masses, the Trail of the Ledges begins as another easy walk, but quickly accelerates up the mountainside. Soon the trail compares with the steepest paths found in the Berkshires. Rough and formidable rock faces with almost vertical layering reveal the mountain's twisted and tough geologic character. Slightly metamorphosed during past mountain-building events, the rocks reveal their slates, schists and mica with growing regularity.

The trail continues its unrelenting climb until hitting the mountain's backbone. Now well above the valley, the forest changes, with patches of sky glimmering through the low, thin canopy. A small viewpoint peers back to the east, focusing on October State Forest to the southeast. Oaks and birch line the mountainside view. Also visible is 2,177-foot Beckett Mountain. The trail wanders along the ridge, moving into a drier forest. Soon more fire-adapted species, including mountain laurel, red maple, and American chestnut, begin to dominate the forest, yet the relatively fertile bedrock and favorable topography allow a more diverse forest to grow. Cool dark hemlocks escort the trail in places, while a few trillium decorate the forest floor in others.

A bend in the trail delivers a small view to the north, focused on the upper Housatonic River and its accompanying mountain valleys. The mountain silhouettes distinctly reveal the region's glacially derived U-shaped contours. Continuing, the trail dips into a small, sheltered valley that holds more moisture than the surrounding forest. Rich green and copper color the land, which supports a more diverse and lush community. Once above the depression, the trail climbs a short, steep face, moving through sunny woodlands populated by blackberries, red oak, and chestnut oak. The trail undulates a bit, but the route is generally easy as it heads for the summit. Windy and battered by winter storms, the local tree cover is low, but the relatively fertile soils produce healthy trees.

Dunbar Road Approach

An easier, but less diverse, option for ascending Lenox Mountain begins at the crest of Dunbar Road as it crosses the Stockridge-Lenox Mountain ridgetop. The route lacks the ponds and wildlife of the Stockbridge Valley, but the hike is much easier and about the same distance. Starting at an elevation of slightly more than 1,600 feet reduces the amount of climb by more than half. Also, since Pleasant Valley Wildlife Sanctuary does not allow dogs, this route allows canine friends to accompany hikers, and there is no access fee.

The trail, an old dirt road following the crest of Lenox Mountain all the way to the Bromley Ski Area, provides accesses to the entire ridgetop. Surrounded by second-growth forest of oak, birch, beech and hemlock, along with lesser amounts of another dozen tree species, the route is attractive and tame. Tall second-growth forest and an uncluttered understory produce an inviting scene. Lively small streams and lush wetland areas cross and escort the path. Although charming during most of the year, in times of high water the route can degrade

The view from Yokun Seat is as impressive as the view from Lenox Mountain is disappointing.

into a muddy, almost impassible, corridor. Some of the wet areas persist year-round, but they do not pose much of an obstacle.

The poor drainage is the result of glacial scouring and subsequent till deposition. The impermeable bedrock traps the water, which cannot escape. About two-thirds of the way to the summit, the trail merges with a larger dirt road and passes a couple of houses. The route continues north. All the while, the mountain's shoulder to the east continues to climb before merging with the summit. The shoulder holds the trail climbing up from the Pleasant Valley Wildlife Sanctuary.

The trail's only challenging stretch is near the summit, where it climbs Lenox's final 200 feet. In this area the trail divorces the dirt road for a short period, making more of a beeline for the summit. Once at the summit, the dirt road and trails all converge by the fire tower.

At the Summit

Lenox Mountain's summit is not isolated, nor wild. It is ugly. It is a disappointment. The decrepit fire tower is a battered skeleton. Its metal bones tear into the sky supporting nothing but their own sorrowful weight. A rusty, partially toppled barbed wire fence surrounds the fire tower and its sterile surroundings. The fence is without purpose, its gate torn away and the accompanying barbed wire within reach of children. The rusty, tangled wire separates from the fence in places, perhaps reaching for the healthier ground around it. On the ground, crushed stone and broken glass coat the mountain. A few telephone poles climbing the mountain's western face cast harsh shadows, their crisscrosses of wires making visual trip wires. A scarred park bench interrupts the bedrock, waiting for people that might want to stay here and enjoy this messy scene.

To the south, a wide dirt road cuts through the heavy mountaintop forest like a stripe on a skunk. Only a few steps along this bold route reveal another poorly fenced area, holding a small herd of radio and satellite towers. Overgrown with grasses and shrubs, the pen is a mountaintop version of an unkempt alley. A few of the towers have individual fences as well. In a teasing manner, a slice of what could be a great view opens to the south and southwest. Most of the higher peaks in the southern Berkshires dot the landscape. Monument Mountain, East Mountain, Mount Everett, Bash Bish Mountain and Alander Mountain are among the most prominent peaks. To the southwest rise the Catskills; their soft shapes and rounded peaks lift along the horizon, the gently curved peaks a good example of how glaciers round and smooth landscapes.

Luckily, a couple of hundred feet to the north, a few open fields filled with grasses and low-lying blueberries provide a more natural and pleasant setting. Here, with only the fire tower's skeletal crown visible above a ring of oak and birch shield, there is a better viewing experience. It is not as extensive as the view from the summit, but it is a more rewarding scene.

Although this view is an improvement over the summit area, there is little reason to linger; this view pales compared to what lies about a half mile to the north. The old roadbed, while not as well defined, keeps to the top of the ridge and displays a confusing series of red, blue and yellow markings. The route leads through a crowded forest of oak, birch, cherry, beech and hemlock toward Yokun Seat, the true gem of Lenox Mountain. The walk is easy, with only small changes in elevation. Mud is often the toughest aspect of the walk. Picking out the route that remains along the top can be a bit tricky, especially with all the different colored markings on the trees, but the main trail is generally wide and easy to follow. To stray more than a few feet from the main trail will lead into thick forest or sharply downhill.

Yokun Seat is only about twenty feet lower than Lenox Mountain's summit. Although there is a tower on Yokun Seat, it is little more than a telephone pole. The pole stands out imposingly from Lenox Mountain and even from the neighboring valleys, but once on-site the structure is much less imposing, supporting only a radio repeater. The occasional vocal outburst can be a bit startling on this less-visited rise, but the sound and the pole are not particularly obtrusive, and the breathtaking view quickly takes center stage—along with stage left and right as well. To enjoy this mountain drama, Yokun Seat offers expansive grassy clearings along with comfortable rock sitting platforms. Open, unhindered views extend for almost three-quarters of the compass rose.

The only direction not open to viewing is south, where the messy Lenox mountaintop lies behind thick tree cover. To the north rises Mount Greylock, its elevation and mass enhanced by the low, wide Housatonic Valley. A product of glacial Lake Housatonic, the valley is much wider than what the present-day Housatonic could create. To the north is the former basin of glacial Lake Bascom. Together these two former lake beds create the low interludes between the mountain masses. As western Massachusetts' premier landmark, Greylock's 3,491-foot peak captures and holds the eye's attention. From this viewing angle, the family of small crests and peaks composing Greylock's massive rise shows up as a complex series of folds and ridges. In the foreground are Pittsfield and Pontoosuc Lake. The land then rises up to form Lenox Mountain, first cresting at the Brodie Mountain ski area. Across the sharp valley and to the east rises the Hoosac Range. This unheralded set of mountains crosses the Vermont state line and geographically transforms into the well-known Green Mountains. The Hoosac rocks lie atop the older Berkshire rocks. Farther east are the low masses of the uncapped Berkshires.

West of Greylock rises the Taconic Mountains' backbone, Misery Mountain. The 2,818-foot Berlin Mountain anchors the range. Beyond them rise additional Taconic peaks in southwestern Vermont and New York. Once again the glacial lake beds create the foreground, enhancing the scene's elevational contrast. Wetlands are another product on the former lake beds, with a large one sitting west of the viewpoint.

As the mountain ridges race to the south and begin to slip behind the local tree cover, the almost 4,000-foot peaks of the northern Catskills surge above the lower Taconic ridges. Although forty miles away, the Catskills rise as an impressive visual cornerstone beyond the lower, nearer Taconic ridgelines. Within the Catskills, the 3,990-foot Blackhead Range forms a distinctive triple peak. To their right rises the lower summit of 3,524-foot Windham Mountain. The high, rounded mountain forms lift as a reminder that not all of the wilderness lies north of Massachusetts.

The return trip to the summit of Lenox Mountain and its un-inviting peak traces the same route used to reach Yokun Seat. From there, retracing either route ends the hike, but the wildlife sanctuary offers many additional walking trails. Lenox Mountain is one of the most stunning hikes in the Taconics, from both a positive and a nega-tive perspective. With the relatively easy drive to Dunbar Road and the relatively nontaxing hike from this access, it also has one of the great-est effort-to-reward ratios in western Massachusetts. ⋏

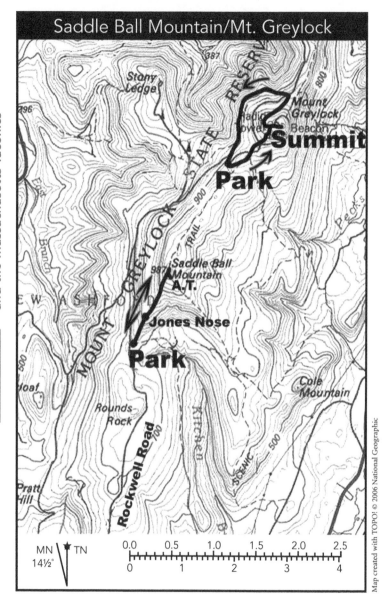

Map created with TOPO! © 2006 National Geographic

Saddle Ball Mountain

Highlight: View from Jones Nose

> **Hike Length:** 2.1 miles round trip
> **Hike Difficulty:** Easy to moderate
> **Starting Elevation:** 2,353'
> **Highest Elevation:** 3,238'

Directions:

US 7 to N. Main St., about 1 mile north of Sumner St. in Pittsfield. Take N. Main St. east for .6 miles to Greylock Rd. (right). Follow Greylock Rd. .4 miles to Rockwell Rd. Follow Rockwell Rd. (pass visitor center) for about 5 miles to Jones Nose Trail parking area on right.

GPS

Jones Nose Parking:	42°36.09; 73°12.03
Saddle Ball Summit:	42°36.82; 73°11.51

At 3,238 feet, Saddle Ball Mountain is the second-highest peak in Massachusetts and the state's highest undeveloped summit. Crossed by the AT (Appalachian Trail), the mountain receives many visitors, most of whom miss one of the state's grandest views. Southwest of the main summit, Jones Nose is a smaller promontory of Saddle Ball Mountain, but its view to the southwest stretches south along the Taconics and over to the Catskills. Framed and fanned by fragrant balsam fir trees, the open and relatively level rock platform forms a grand stage.

The Jones Nose Trail to Saddle Ball Mountain begins on the east side of Rockwell Road, 2.7 miles north of the Mount Greylock visitors center. Heading north, the trail cuts through a hedge before entering a large field with introductory versions of the mountain's far-reaching views. The main line of the Taconic ridge fills the middle ground to the south and west. The nearby hills, a combination of Taconic and Berkshire varieties, spread out in a wide southern arc. Altogether, the landscape knits a scene akin to a Massachusetts version of *The Sound of Music.* Poor air quality often limits this view, with gray and brown haze dissolving the distant ridges in atmospheric filth. Still, the greens and golds of the surrounding fields dance in mesmerizing patterns, and splashes of wildflowers enhance the scene. A few maple and birch trees lift above the field, their ball-shaped crowns spreading wide because there is no competition for light.

The blue-marked trail is easy to follow as it winds through the field and heads toward the steeper, forested mountain. The line between field and forest is distinct, and on sunny days the temperature can drop significantly once in the shade. The trail becomes rocky and much steeper as it heads into the northern hardwood forest. A thick canopy of maple, beech, birch and cherry about forty feet high slows the wind. Drops of sunlight dapple the understory of blackberry, hobblebush, fern, and beech saplings. In thick patches, the blackberries dominate this understory and make for a great late-summer treat. Summer's asters add a touch of brighter colors to the forest greens and earthy browns and grays. Although the forest is maturing on these slopes, the presence of blackberries, ferns and asters is a sure sign that these slopes, like the fields below, were recently open as well.

After pushing up an initial slope, the trail begins to level off somewhat, but retains a general upward climb. In places, puddles, mud and even small wetlands persist as the trail winds through these once-glaciated lands. When the ice reshaped the land and deposited the materials in the melting ice, poor drainage resulted.

Once up the first major incline, the trail then passes the CCC (Civilian Conservation Corps) Dynamite foot and ski trail about a

Jones Nose offers one of the most impressive Taconic views, and the open fields provide a unique perspective.

half mile below the AT junction. After the junction, the trail continues to climb at a regular, but not overly difficult, pace. Stiff-needled red spruce join the forest, adding a darker element to the foliage. With more gaps in the canopy, the forest opens and shadows dissipate, but no views unfold. Next appears balsam fir, another major mountaintop tree in the Appalachians. With the onset of the more alpine ecosystem, the telltale dark organic soils become apparent, along with standing water.

A few steps west of the trail, a spectacular viewpoint to the south and west opens and easily ranks amongst the Taconics' finest panoramas. Spending a few minutes to enjoy this vista is well worth the delay. In the distance rises the low, but solid, Shawangunk ridge. Farther west and north rise the Catskill Mountains. Even that range's highest peak, 4,180-foot Slide Mountain, makes an appearance. Slide's summit is the highest point visible from the Taconics and is 1,500 feet higher than Jones Nose. Closer in the western viewshed stretch Brodie Mountain, Jiminy Peak, and Misery Mountain. To the south, 2,602-foot Mount Everett stands out as the king of the southern Taconics. Lakes and ski trails provide convenient orientation beacons. To the east, the Berkshires' low mountain wall rises where mountain ash reclaims the horizon. Once up those rounded slopes, the Berkshire summits stretch away in plateau-like fashion.

Once above the viewpoint, the spruce-fir forest becomes better established. Balsam freshens the air, and soon balsam fir trees replace red spruce. Winter's harshness dominates the forest's growing patterns, and many twisted and dwarfed trees cover the slopes. As part of Massachusetts' highest island of elevation, this area meets incoming weather patterns without the benefit of surrounding landforms to temper the atmosphere's angry blows. As a result, snow, wind and ice can relentlessly pummel the exposed slopes.

Again the trail levels off, and then intersects the 2,100-plus-mile AT, which heads north to Maine and south to Georgia. To the north, Greylock's summit is 2.6 miles away. The intersection lies atop Saddle Ball Mountain's main ridge. Strong white quartz veins, a product of the rock's metamorphic past, help support the summit. A thick and healthy spruce-fir forest, well established here at a relatively low elevation, covers the summit. Oxalis and bunchberry dot the dark understory.

Although the trail heads directly for Mount Greylock, the trail and the road become entwined, which detracts from the serene wilds atop Saddle Ball Mountain. Rather than continuing on, the hike is more impressive when returning to the views and fields of the Jones

Nose Trail. Before returning down the blue-marked trail, continue south on the AT for about one-tenth of a mile to another viewpoint. Facing the east and north, this vista is not as expansive as the one on the Jones Nose trail, but it reveals an entirely different scene, anchored by some of southern New England's most recognizable summits including Mount Monadnock and Mount Wachusett. Although low, the jagged ridgeline of Mount Tom shows clearly against the horizon. The view extends across the Berkshires over the sunken Connecticut River Valley, and then reveals small pieces of the Worcester Hills. To the southeast, the view drifts toward the Litchfield Hills.

On returning to the Jones Nose Trail, the downhill walk is steep in places, but quiet and pleasant. The trail's scenery continues to reward the eyes. Soon the forest yields to the open fields, and the open fields to the parking area. From here, a drive toward Mount Greylock provides access to another great hike. ⚡

Mount Greylock (see map on page 24)

Highlight: View from the war memorial tower

> **Hike Length:** 2.25-mile loop
> **Hike Difficulty:** Easy to moderate
> **Starting Elevation:** 3,024'
> **Highest Elevation:** 3,491'

Directions:

US 7 to N. Main St., about 1 mile north of Sumner St. in Pittsfield. Take N. Main St. east for .6 miles to Greylock Rd. (right). Follow Greylock Rd. .4 miles to Rockwell Rd. Follow Rockwell Rd. (pass visitor center) for about 8.5 miles to Appalachian Trail parking area (lot is at bend of second hairpin turn).

GPS

Summit Parking:	42°37.86; 73°10.70
Summit:	42°38.23; 73°09.97

The war memorial tower rising from Mount Greylock is among the most visible and well-known landmarks in Massachusetts. The mountain, which towers above its neighbors, is distinctive in its own right. Its eastern face displays a huge scar from a 1901 landslide. Atop the 3,491-foot mountain rises the Bay State's monument to its war veterans. Crested by a glass globe that shines for seventy miles, the monument evokes thoughts of coastal New England, not of a mountaintop. The structure appears like, and indeed is, a lighthouse. Originally, the monument was to stand guard in the Charles River estuary, but through legislative genius its location—but not its design—changed to Mount Greylock.

Reaching Greylock's summit and lighthouse is easy—perhaps too easy. With a New England tradition of access for all, the thirteen-mile Rockwell Road crosses the mountain massif from Lanesborough to North Adams and provides access to the cleared, tamed summit. Still, the road is not without its merits. At Rockwell Road's southern terminus is a visitor center, and the road also provides a scenic route over the mountain.

Numerous options for approaching Greylock's summit range from a drive up Rockwell Road to a long hike up the Appalachian Trail (AT). Finding the right compromise that visits as much of the summit and its natural highlights, while avoiding the road, cars and the crowds congregating at the summit, creates a more natural Greylock experience.

One of the best choices starts at the parking area above the hairpin turn, seven miles north of the visitor center on Rockwell Road. Here, the AT drops off of Saddle Ball Mountain before lifting again toward Greylock. Together with the Overlook Trail, the route forms a 2.25-mile loop.

On the AT, the route dives into the thick spruce-fir forest, with hobblebush and small beech gaps rounding out the high elevation forest. The beech provide a year-round contrast with dark evergreens. In spring and summer the beech's light green leaves lighten the dark and shadowy forest. In fall the yellow and copper tones deliver a sharp contrast to the seasonally indifferent evergreens. Thick beds of young balsam fir and stubby club mosses cover the ground. As the trail descends from a small knob, it reveals a glimpse of Greylock, and then crosses Rockwell Road. Keeping the paved interruption to a minimum, the trail quickly returns to the thick forest.

The trail soon reaches a small pond with a cabin and a view toward Greylock's towers—both the stone monument and a tall, slender, red and white radio tower. After about a quarter-mile, the trail dives to meet Rockwell Road at its intersection with Summit Drive. The junction includes a cadre of road signs directing cars to and from the summit. The trail seems lost among the intersection. The forest across the road is inviting.

As the AT climbs Greylock's summit, the trail steepens and slips uncomfortably into a small eroded ravine. An older spruce-fir forest surrounds the trail here, adding heavier shadows to the landscape. Cars and people rarely fade from sight or hearing. The trail's challenge seems welcome compared to the fight to maintain a sense of the wild. The battle is lost for good when the trail emerges at the radio tower and becomes a paved road. Off to the west (left), the Overlook Trail begins a hasty retreat from the developed mountaintop.

Still, it is the mountaintop and its view that beckons, even as the forest gives way to grassy fields, roads, parking areas, monuments, antennas and even a lodge. Three views are worth noting from the summit—an open view to the east, the westward view from the lodge and the 360-degree view from the lighthouse.

The open view to the east is the more natural of Greylock's views, although the view to the west and southwest from Bascom Lodge has an indoor glory of its own. The lodge replaces an older, inadequate building that burned down just before the Great Depression. The state allocated funds to replace the original building, and the effort was then taken over by the Civilian Conservation Corps in the mid-1930s.

Surrounded by other mountain ranges, Mount Greylock's viewshed is among the most diverse in North America. Along the northeastern horizon run the building masses of the White Mountains. A few outliers such as 3,400-foot Mount Monadnock and Mount Wachusett in central Massachusetts stand above the distant range. More to the north are the Green Mountains in Vermont, anchored by 3,990-foot Stratton Mountain. As this range heads south it blends into its lower geologic cousins—first the Hoosac Range,

The view from Greylock tower, which is both a monument and a light-house, offers a 360-degree view.

and then the Berkshire Hills, which rise directly east of Greylock. In the southeast the range dissolves into the lower Litchfield Hills in Connecticut. Directly north and south and west of Greylock run its Taconic brethren. To the north, and mainly out of view, rise the kings of the range, Equinox and Dorset. To the west is the mountain wall of Misery Mountain, capped by the 2,818-foot summit of Berlin Mountain. Far beyond them to the northwest are the southern Adirondack summits. To the southeast rise the Catskills, a mass of 3,500-foot peaks. The Catskills' Slide Mountain, at 4,180 feet, is the highest point visible from Mount Greylock. Slicing south of the

Catskills is the Shawangunk Ridge, composed of extremely hard sediments eroded from the ancestral Taconic Mountains.

Greylock's summit is wet, and the high precipitation and cool temperatures result in abundant moisture. While the neighboring valleys receive forty-five inches of precipitation per year, the mountaintop's bold foray into the atmosphere brings it an additional ten inches. Snowfall on Greylock averages seventy inches. So, while the soils may be shallow, rocky and infertile, water is often readily available and competition for sunlight is minimal. Along with spruce and fir, yellow birch and hobblebush can thrive in this rugged environment.

Picking a descent route from Greylock that keeps the roads and development at bay is not an easy task. Overall, the Overlook Trail provides the best course. Heading downhill quickly, the blue-marked Overlook Trail flees the highly developed summit. The trail begins near the maintenance area and its red and white radio antenna. Fortunately, the spruce-fir forest quickly screens travelers from the unnatural mountaintop scene. Fresh balsam and cool breezes replace heavy exhaust and constant chatter. Soft mosses replace the hard asphalt. As soon as the trail begins to lose elevation, tree heights increase. Quickly, beech and birch become more important forest components.

Continuing to lose elevation, the trail abruptly encounters and crosses the Rockwell Road. Once across the road, the trail skirts the top edge of the Hopper, an area among the most remote and rugged in the state. Paralleling the road, the rocky path punishes knees and ankles. At one point a short spur trail heads to the west, providing a pleasant sliver of a view to the northwest peering upon the Taconic Range as it enters Vermont. Then the trail moves farther downhill into forests better protected from the elements. Beech trees increase in size and numbers. Stream crossings abound, the largest of which, in about a quarter of a mile downstream, boldly dives off the mountain as March Cataract Falls.

For its final length the route heads steeply uphill to rejoin Rockwell Road as it makes a hairpin turn. The parking area is only a few hundred feet uphill along the road. The open roadway gathers additional warmth on sunny days, but lacks the ability to keep the mountain's stiff breezes at bay.

Although a bit chaotic, hiking on and around Massachusetts' highest peaks is worth the effort and cannot be ignored by anyone wanting to explore the Taconics. In addition, the ability to drive to the top when short on time or energy provides an enjoyable experience unique to southern New England. ⋏

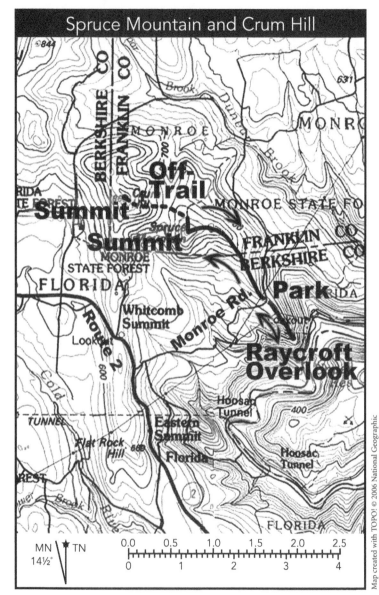

Spruce Mountain and Crum Hill

Spruce Mountain and Crum Hill

Highlight: View from Raycroft Overlook

> **Hike Length:** 4.6 miles round trip (an additional .8 miles round trip to Raycroft Overlook)
> **Hike Difficulty:** Moderate
> **Starting Elevation:** 2,050'
> **Highest Elevation:** 2,841'

Directions:

MA Route 2 to Whitcomb Hill Rd., which is about 2.5 miles east of a hairpin turn above North Adams. Head north on Whitcomb Hill Rd. for .1 miles. Bear left on Monroe Rd. (becomes dirt) for about 2 miles. Park at junction of Monroe Rd. with dirt road on right.

GPS

Parking:	42°41.65; 73°59.21
Spruce Summit:	42°42.31; 72°00.33
Crum Summit:	42°42.63; 73°01.17
Raycroft Overlook:	42°41.33; 72°58.90

As Vermont's Green Mountains reach south, they lose much of their stature. Their name disappears from maps at the Massachusetts border, but the Green Mountains have not come to an end. The Hoosac Range is a southern extension of the Green Mountains. Although elevationally poorer than their Green relatives, the Hoosac Range is one of the highest areas of Massachusetts. The range's two highest peaks—Crum Hill, the highest point in Franklin County, and Spruce Mountain, the second-highest peak—roll into relative obscurity as they hide among similarly rounded hills and receive little attention. Both peaks are easily visible from the Mohawk Trail, yet it is the towers on mighty Greylock that draw the eye and tourist. In addition, Crum Hill, at 2,841 feet, is the highest point in the state not located on the Mount Greylock massif.

Spruce Mountain rises within Massachusetts' Monroe State Forest. The trail begins along Monroe Road at its junction with the route to the Raycroft Overlook. The blue-marked Spruce Hill Trail heads west, immediately diving into a thick and healthy second-growth forest. After a few steps through this comfortable beech-dominated forest, the trees part as the trail crosses a clearing for a set of tripled power lines. Exposed to sunlight and wind, this open area has a more extreme climate. Ferns and blackberries form a thick and prickly cover beneath this electric skyway.

Soon back amongst the natural forest cover, the trail moves through a northern hardwood forest. The smooth silvery beech bark is often spoiled by the ravages of beech bark disease. Broken, scarred and black patches mar the normally smooth bark. Sugar maple and yellow birch are other common trees. Along the ground is a generous coating of ferns with bracken, with ferns among the most common. It is a pleasant second-growth forest. Good specimens of black cherry, which can be worth thousands of dollars each to the timber industry, stand out among the forest. The first sporadic patch of red spruce joins the forest as well.

As for most of the hike up Spruce Mountain, the trail lends itself to a moderate pace. The migration from Berkshire to Franklin County passes without ceremony. Set near the 2,400-foot line, the geographical change is merely a line on a map—meaningless within this northern hardwood forest. Keeping to the path of least resistance up the mountainside, the trail follows the southeastern shoulder. A healthy second-growth forest surrounds the trail, bringing a cheery green to the landscape. Birch, beech and maple are the most common residents. Commercially logged in the past, these slopes produced valuable timber, and the old timber roads provide the basis for the area's trail system. The wider berth needed for logging equipment prevents the trail from being more intimate with the surrounding forest and creates a sun-drenched strip along the route, supporting a variety of grasses, ferns, wildflowers and berries atypical of the forest interior.

A little before the trail approaches the mountain's 2,600-foot eastern summit, a charming view opens to the south. Small mountains, rolling ridgelines and steep valleys portray a rugged region quite uninviting to the eighteenth-century American hungry for farmland and easy transportation. The whole of the Berkshires was settled much later—more than a century in many cases—than the surrounding Connecticut and Hudson valleys.

In contrast, today's visitors come specifically for the mountains' wild character and challenging terrain. The view spans the scenic Mohawk Trail as it climbs the canyon-like Deerfield Valley and crosses the Hoosac Range. The view then stretches more than fifty miles to the south to 2,602-foot Mount Everett, whose dome shape pokes above the lower, closer ridgeline. Located only a few miles from Vermont, the view stretches almost to the Connecticut line, tracing what is nearly the entire width of Massachusetts. A frame built of northern red oaks, beech and a few spruce limits the view. The melted, metamorphic rock reveals the frozen plastic patterns generated under the tremendous heat and pressure this rock encountered when it was buried miles below the earth's surface.

Hobblebush is a major understory component. In spring, its white flowers brighten the brown and gray forest, while in autumn the ruddy leaves mute the late-season color. The trail then crosses Spruce Mountain's eastern summit and drops into a small gap before rising the final 170 feet. The trail becomes steeper as it nears the mountaintop, but the climb is short and not overly taxing. Ferns, hobblebush

The Deerfield River Valley provides some of the most spectacular scenery in northwestern Massachusetts.

and blackberry compete with the trees for summit dominance. Although not too high, the increased elevation brings harsher winter conditions, as seen in the slightly stunted birch, oaks and maples at the top. The summit has a limited view to the south, but it is much less interesting than the view from the eastern summit. Once arriving at the mountaintop, the trail turns to the north and begins its descent.

The thick mountaintop vegetation complicates finding the best starting point for the bushwhack toward Crum Hill. When the leaves are out, it is a challenge even to see Crum Hill's outline, much less to determine the best crossover point. Luckily, the terrain is easy to navigate, and almost any direct course to the 2,380-foot notch separating the two peaks provides a reasonable route. The hike down Spruce Mountain's western slopes is easy, with the trip wire-like branches of hobblebush only an occasional nuisance. Within the sheltered notch, straight and tall beech and spruce trunks form natural columns. An old road passes through the notch, its good condition a reminder of how little true wilderness remains in the eastern United States.

From the notch to the summit, the climb gains 460 feet in just over a half-mile, enough to make the trek a good workout. Lifting from the notch, Crum Hill's eastern face is dominated by beech, their yellow-green leaves giving the forest a bright, airy atmosphere. The slope is steeper than on Spruce Mountain, but there is less hobble-bush to impede progress and bruise shins. The upslope route is easy to choose, as the mountain's natural lines provide the shortest, albeit steepest, route toward the summit.

A little south of Crum Hill's summit is a small clearing surround-ed by an orchard of squat yellow birch trees. The clearing provides a tease of a view. For the view to be fully revealed, visitors must climb one of the bronze-trunked trees. Even with the improved perspective, the scene is less extensive than from Spruce Mountain. A few dozen yards south and west of the clearing runs a wide, orange-marked road climbing Crum Hill from the southwest. The true summit lies along the top ridge, which the road parallels, but never fully ascends. When approaching from Spruce Mountain, the road lies on the opposite side of the summit ridge and is only encountered once topping Crum Hill's top contour. A little-visited sign-in canister estimates the top, which is also the highest elevation in Franklin County.

The return route merely traces the path taken to reach the two peaks. The off-trail hike back into the notch and up Spruce Mountain is complicated only by the extensive stands of hobblebush on Spruce Mountain. Refinding the marked trail is simple, as it runs atop the ridgeline heading north from Spruce Mountain. As a result, any reasonable eastward course will successfully deliver the trail.

One nice feature about hiking to Spruce Mountain and Crum Hill is a short bonus hike to the Raycroft Overlook. Perched on a stone platform above the Deerfield Valley, the view takes in much of Franklin County and the high points in southeastern Vermont and southwestern New Hampshire. The steep drop into canyon-like Deerfield Valley is among the most dramatic viewsheds in the Berkshires. A power-storing reservoir sits atop the canyon wall. Like a spider web, gossamer power lines overlay much of the landscape, a potent intrusion upon the mostly unbroken forests.

The power lines also once served the controversial Yankee-Rowe Nuclear Plant, New England's first commercial reactor. Brought on line in 1961, the plant generated up to 185 megawatts of electricity. The facility closed in 1991, ten years before scheduled, because of its deteriorating infrastructure. Located on the eastern side of the river, some structures remain and physical, economic and social impacts from the plant linger within the valley. The neighboring Bear Swamp hydroelectric project can generate up to 660 megawatts of power, but requires energy inputs for replenishment.

Located east of the trailhead to Spruce Mountain, the trail begins as a dirt road leading to a set of high-tension wires. The open area around the towers provides a view into the central Berkshires and a peek at the tower on Mount Greylock. At this point the road quickly degrades into a wide path and begins the steep descent into the Deerfield Valley. Hemlock stands bring a cool, dark character to the land, a stark contrast with the blasted landscape under the towers. Although the rise back from the overlook is the most intensive of the entire hike, the rewarding view is more than worth the effort and makes for a delightful short trip of its own. ⚘

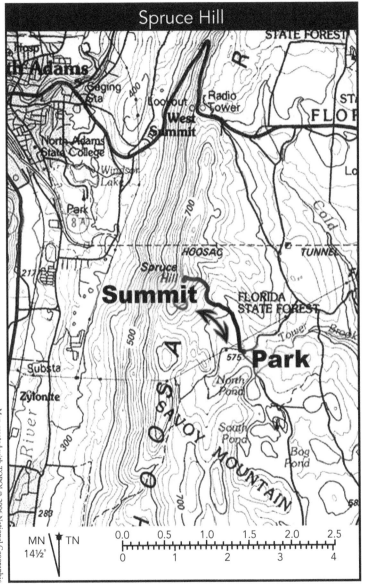

Spruce Hill

Highlight: View from the cliffs

Hike Length: 2.6 miles round trip
Hike Difficulty: Easy to moderate
Starting Elevation: 1,865'
Highest Elevation: 2,566'

Directions:

MA 2 to Central Shaft Rd., which is 1.6 miles east of the hairpin turn above North Adams. Go south on Central Shaft Rd. for about 1.5 miles. Parking area is on right by a sharp curve and junction with a dirt road.

GPS

Parking:	42° 39.48; 73° 03.35
Summit:	42° 40.20; 73° 04.14

The Hoosac Range forms the Hoosic and Stockbridge valleys' eastern edge, creating a formidable mountain wall mirroring the Taconic Range to the west. Capped by thrust-faulted schists and lying atop Grenville gneiss, the Hoosac rocks sit atop their billion-year-old Berkshire cousins. The faulted rocks give the Hoosac Range an elevational boost. South and east of the Hoosacs, masses of uncapped Grenville-rock hills spread to the horizon. To the north, the Hoosacs merge into the higher Green Mountains. Mount Greylock and its subordinates dominate the western sky and eclipse much of the range's status. Spruce Hill in Savoy State Forest is a representative example—the mountain rises to 2,566 feet and is one of the state's higher summits, yet it only bears the label "hill."

The trail to Spruce Hill begins at a bend in the Savoy Center Road, a little north of a public use and fishing area. The first few feet of trail use the Old Florida Road, a muddy dirt track that is more of a collection of ruts than a navigable surface. Fortunately, the right turn onto the blue-marked Busby Trail occurs quickly. The land rises gently. The poorly drained trail, a product of erosion and glacial sculpting, is often muddy, especially in spring. The land is heavily wooded, but the forest is not old—the area was used for farmland, pastureland and timbering until the early 1900s. The recovering forest is dominated by northern red oak, yellow birch and paper birch.

After a quarter mile, the first of two power lines slices the trail. Utility companies keep the area open, and on sunny days the clearing is often much warmer than the surrounding forest. As a result, the extremes in moisture and temperature influence what grows best. If it was not regularly cleared, the forest would return. The first tree species to grow here would be those best adjusted for high light, along with temperature and moisture swings. In general this favors poplars, oaks and pines—pioneer species.

The trail continues to head gently uphill over the next quarter mile. Sunk into the eroded landscape, the trail is bordered by countless exposed roots, many dead from exposure. Stands of Norway spruce, commonly planted for reforestation during and after the Great Depression, darken the trail and forest floor. Like a parade ground full of soldiers, the green and brown trees stand in orderly rows. Such regularity is somewhat disturbing among nature's randomness, yet it is less out of character so near the wide power-line cuts.

A wide, bright opening introduces a second set of power lines, the high-tension wires floating between large steel towers. The lines ignore the Berkshires' landscape, climbing up and down the mountainsides oblivious to the terrain. Down one mountainside and up the next, the wide swath is free of high vegetation. The result is a cross section through the mountains' skin and into their rocky bones. The forest alongside the power lines is dominated by American beech, their smooth slivery gray bark lending the forest edge a lustrous quality. Bordering the open ground, the trees along the edge take advantage of the direct sunlight, spreading their branches into the clearing as far as they can reach. Forest trees typically face fierce competition for sunlight; the only way for most of them to get additional light is to grow taller. Here, the trees can reach into the cleared area, gathering more sunlight without growing taller; however, they are more susceptible to wind and ice damage.

The trail then dives back into the forest and begins to climb. A small stream escorts the trail, its water rushing downhill in a miniature torrent of sound. The surrounding forest is a mix of beech, birch, oak and hemlock, with the oak absent from the understory; the young oaks are unable to get enough light in this shady forest. Stone walls slice across the land, and few of the trees are more than eighty years old—sure signs that this is second-growth forest.

Next the trail makes a slight bend to the right and crosses the playful stream. In a unique forest show, paper birch trunks form an almost solid picket of white columns. The view through the forest grabs the eye and is a memorable trail moment.

Soon the forest returns to a mix of maple, beech and birch, and the trail continues its steady climb. An old foundation, well-built and a reminder of the area's past use for agriculture, marks another turn in the trail. A large yellow birch tree inhabits the old foundation, its age a testament to the passage of time.

After the foundation, the trail becomes steeper. The forest remains diverse, with some hemlock and spruce sharing the area with the northern hardwoods. Soon the Busby Trail intersects the Long Pond Trail, which heads south and makes a part of the loop back to the Old Florida Road. The route, however, is not overly scenic—only longer

A great short hike, Spruce Hill offers a good view to the north and west.

and much muddier. The Busby Trail continues uphill, with beech trees dominating the forest. Copper beech leaves coat the ground, and the bright yellow-green living leaves make the forest bright and cheerful.

The forest is generally quiet, and signs of wildlife are scattered. Spring peepers and wild turkey are common noisemakers. Red-eyed vireos enliven the woods in summer. Bears, fox and deer also move through this forest. During spring and fall migrations, hawks are a common sight.

After crossing another trail, the route continues to pick its way along increasingly uneven ground, the land eagerly rising into the Hoosac Range's upper reaches. A few oak and birch trees mix into the forest.

The metamorphic rock, mainly Hoosac schist, reveals its melted and deformed character as belts of distorted colors and layers. Hoosac schist is an old rock, dating back to Precambrian and Cambrian times. Originally, the materials composing most of the Hoosac Range developed on an ancient continental slope. Micas in the schist—muscovite, chlorite and biotite—give this rock its sparkle. Small garnet, and large .75-inch white and black crystals of albite feldspar add to the rock's varied appearance. Layers of marble and amphibolite mix with the schist to make a complex bedrock structure.

A series of steps and a short, steep climb deliver the trail to the summit, which offers two spectacular viewpoints. The first looks north and northwest into Vermont's Green Mountains, while the Berkshires lift to the east. To the west, North Adams sits in the gap between Mount Greylock and the Green Mountains. Farther west are Williamstown, the Taconic Range and Mount Greylock. Clarksburg Mountain, the most southerly point in the Green Mountains, sneaks over the state line and into Massachusetts. The southerly viewpoint is more open, set on a knife-like rock fin. To the north and south, the view follows the north-south axis of the Hoosac Range, the eye cruising along this impressive mountain wall. A fifty-foot cliff masks the summit to the south and overlooks a dwarfed beech, birch and oak forest. Most of the trees have wide crowns, almost like species-specific tufts of cotton candy. The view includes the southern Berkshires and the Taconics, Mount Greylock and even the distant Catskills. To the southeast a fire tower tops Borden Mountain. Leafless seasons present a limited view to the east, where the Berkshire Hills spread out in a gentle sea of low mountains.

The return trip is easy; the best route is to retrace the initial ascent. A longer, often swampy route that would complete a loop begins by turning right (south) at the trail junction just below the summit. On the return trip, the trail is easy to navigate, and the land is gentle enough not to bother ankles or knees.

Set along the crest and arguably the most impressive Hoosac vista, Spruce Hill is an important landmark and hike among the region's summits. Although not often recognized or even noticed, the Hoosac Range marks the transition between the Taconics, Greens and Berkshires, and this small set of mountains has a geologic identity of its own. Hiking Spruce Hill helps bring newfound respect for this often overlooked spine of western Massachusetts. ⚹

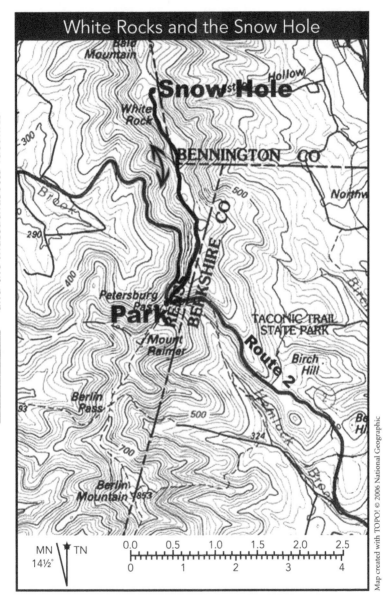

White Rocks and the Snow Hole

The Northern Berkshires, the Hoosac Range and the Massachusetts Taconics

50

Bald Mountain

Snow Hole

Hollow

White Rock

BENNINGTON CO

Brook

300

290

400

Petersburg Pass

Park

Mount Raimer

Berlin Pass

93

Berlin Mountain 1853

BERKSHIRE CO

500

Northw

TACONIC TRAIL STATE PARK

Route 2

Birch Hill

Hemlock

500

324

700

Birch Brook

Be Hi

Brook

MN 14½°

TN

0.0   0.5   1.0   1.5   2.0   2.5

0   1   2   3   4

Map created with TOPO! © 2006 National Geographic

White Rocks and the Snow Hole

Highlight: Snow in July!

> **Hike Length**: 5.4 miles
> **Hike Difficulty:** Easy to moderate
> **Starting Elevation:** 2,080'
> **Highest Elevation:** 2,530'

Directions:

> MA/NY 2 to Petersburg Pass, which is .2 miles west of the New York-Massachusetts state border. Parking is on the south side of the road.

GPS

Parking:	42°43.39; 73°16.67
Snow Hole:	42°45.53; 73°16.84

Heading to the Snow Hole in early to mid-summer is like stepping into a horror movie. The sun dims, heavy rock walls seem to close in and silence abounds. The air chills the skin, and a blackness pulls at the living green world. With a few steps into the fissure, each breath spills out as fog. Next, a slick icy world replaces summer's last vestiges and snow crunches underfoot. Cold and dank, this winter retreat persists just below the surface world and its summer glory.

Climbing from the Little Hoosic and Green River valleys, State Route 2 tops the Taconic Ridge at the 2,080-foot Petersburg Pass. A generous parking area fills much of the pass, providing ample, albeit chaotic, parking. The blue-and-white-marked Taconic Crest Trail crosses through the pass and continues north, offering the best route to the Snow Hole. Although the trail comes within 100 feet of Massachusetts, the path never enters the Bay State; however, it traverses the southwesternmost corner of Vermont about a mile and a half into the hike.

The Petersburg Pass provides one of the few paved routes through the Taconics. To the south, the Taconics travel the fifteen-mile ridge-line of Misery Mountain, a long north-south-trending ridge. Along with the geographical barriers presented by state boundaries, this area lagged in commercial development and transportation. As a result, significant portions of the area were able to be preserved, providing needed recreation and natural refuges for wildlife and people.

Once crossing Route 2, the trail immediately heads uphill at a moderate grade. Although steep, the trail barely has time to wind hikers before inviting a pause to enjoy its first view. A grassy area, bordered by a large field of hay-scented ferns, showcases a view to the west. Even without the rest of the hike, this easy-to-access viewpoint is a spectacular place to escape civilization or to enjoy a sunset. The Taconic plateau dominates the view. Farther north, Adirondack foothills form the horizon, but with only a hint of their impressive heights. Below the viewpoint is the Little Hoosic Valley and New York Route 22, a constant Taconic companion.

The trail continues to climb the ridgeline before leveling off at about 2,250 feet. Maps of the area designate much of this land as White Rocks, with the name stretching over the state line into Vermont. The trail is in good condition, free from the deep ruts and large muddy stretches common along the Taconic Crest Trail south of Petersburg Pass. Signs show up with annoying frequency everywhere in these woods. The constant text detracts from the land's character, but still a lush, green world lines the trail. Yellow birch, American beech and northern red oak dominate the forest along with fewer numbers of sugar maple, paper birch, hemlock and white pine—overall, a diverse second-growth forest. Coppiced trees spread over much of the landscape, with a dense mix of grasses, ferns and wildflowers escorting the trail.

The trees on this part of the ridge are large and tall, signs that this area has had decades free from major disturbances. Bronzed trunks of yellow birch gleam in the sunshine. After a little more than a half mile, the trail encounters one of the route's first major landmarks, the Shepherds Well Trail. The blue-marked trail heads east (right). The side trail descends along a ridge through Hopkins Forest into the pass's lower reaches.

The Taconic Crest Trail's grade is gentle, presenting an easy climb as the route rolls along the high Taconics' eastern edge. The trail undulates along the ridge's meandering top contour. Where the trail reaches a gentle crest, the thick dense forests often yield to large fern fields. Heralded by their sweet, pleasant odor, yellow-green hay-scented ferns are the most common variety. In some stands these ferns cover acres of mountaintop. Embedded in the fern fields are taller, circular clusters of interrupted fern. As open fields, they receive more sunlight and are often warmer and drier than the surrounding forest. Closely knit, the ferns keep the trees' progeny at bay and—for the time being at least—sustain themselves on the shallow yet fertile soils.

After about a mile, and after passing the union with a second side trail, the Blue Birch Trail, the route begins a significant climb. Away from ridgetops, the trees are often larger than on the highest elevations. In places, two-foot-diameter trees make for an impressive forest. Sunny fern glades and well-developed second-growth forest present a striking contrast. Throughout the forest, but especially prevalent along this stretch of trail, the rufous-sided towhee's "drink your tea" call is common.

Once atop the modest rise leading to this section of White Rocks, a series of three views unfolds to the south, west and northwest.

Mount Greylock and Mount Raimer dominate the southern view, their glacially rounded and time-softened features well displayed. Farther south of Mount Raimer, the Taconic crest then tops off as the 2,818-foot Berlin Mountain and then continues south along the desolate Misery Mountain. In the west, the Catskills' stalwart front lifts almost 4,000 feet from the Hudson Valley in a distant, yet impressive, mountain display. In reality, these mountains are the easternmost and highest extension of the Allegheny Plateau. North of the Catskills are the Helderbergs, a limestone and dolomite ridge lining the Mohawk Valley's southern flank. North of the Mohawk Valley, the long stretch of rising hills grows into the Adirondack Mountains.

With the trail moving away from the road, the area is quieter. Mountain laurel and azalea are plentiful, adding splashes of white and

pink to the scene. Here, both the eye and ear can celebrate as the first of the three viewpoints greets the trail. The first provides the most extensive view to the southwest, including the best view of Mount Greylock. It also offers the most comfortable seating, making this viewpoint a great place for a snack or lunch. Hemmed in and constricted by encroaching vegetation, the second view stretches out along the trail. The third viewpoint delivers the widest look at the landscape, and its higher elevation adds more perspective to the vista.

Beech trees dominate the forest around and between the views. Known as beech gaps, these almost exclusive communities of beech trees are found throughout the Appalachians. How beech come to so thoroughly dominate slopes typically shared with other northern hardwoods is unknown, but the smooth silvery bark and yellow-green leaves give a fairy-tale quality to the forest. Perhaps the answer lies within the tree's ability to propagate via its roots, sprouting clones at almost regular intervals.

Once beyond this small peak, the trail heads down its steepest slope of the hike as it surges toward the Vermont border, which the trail crosses in about 300 feet. Almost on cue to prepare for entry into the more northerly state, a few red spruce join the forest. After crossing through Vermont for about a quarter mile, the trail reenters New York. Oddly, no signs mark the state-border crossings. After another gentle rise and decline, a red-marked trail, well posted with formal and informal trail signs to the Snow Hole, heads to the east (right). Promising a tough return climb, the new trail continues to yield elevation. A large beech tree heavily scarred with carved initials and declarations of love provides an unfortunate landmark. Most of these wounds will far outlive the love they proclaim. Gouged into the tree's silvery gray skin, the markings

Mount Raimer and Berlin Mountain dominate the view to the south from White Rocks.

remind one of manatee backs—peaceful creatures victimized by forces beyond their understanding.

The landscape around the Snow Hole does little to acknowledge the hole's presence. Little more than another shadow, at first glance, the Snow Hole's dark opening appears like a secret entrance into an ice castle. Shunned by the icons of summer, greens and golds are foreigners here. Like a partial solar eclipse, the Snow Hole's elements of dark and cold bring a false twilight to summer's light and heat, and the longer one stays, the more imposing the feeling becomes.

Stepping into the Snow Hole is like the introductory steps of a journey into the earth. Near the entrance the cool, moist air encourages plant growth. Thick mosses and large trees grow along the Snow Hole's upper fringe. As the gouge burrows into the rock, the shadows darken into blackness and the cool stillness whispers of winters past and those soon to come. Although only a few yards deep, the complicated outline made by the silhouetted fissure lengthens the route. The air becomes still and quiet, like inside a deep cave. To think of slumbering ice dragons and their ilk seems appropriate.

Inside the Snow Hole is a winter shrine. A sense of penetrating cold, snowy landscapes and dormant life is strong. The earth is icy and damp. The smell of decay is omnipresent. Water droplets drip against rocks and wet leaves. The crunch of feet on crushed stone echoes with each step. Then, if it is not too late into summer, the stones give way to a blanket of ice and finally, old snow. Dirty and tainted with litter and gravel, the snow is bound to this place like a monument to the glaciers that once buried these mountains. Now the snow is tired and trapped, imprisoned within dark, wet walls.

Finding snow hidden away in the mountain during the height of summer is a unique experience. Few natural features this far south can harbor a microclimate and microtopography just right for the persistence of snow and ice. Sheltered from sunlight and without an escape route for the cold air, this fascinating locale is one of the Taconics' top curiosities. Without any southern exposure and with a supply of cool air draining from the mountaintops, the well-placed cut into the bedrock is a natural refrigerator. Without a doubt, this spot will be one of the first to harbor a permanent snowfield and then a glacier upon the coming of the next ice age.

The return trip retraces the route to the Snow Hole. As with many trails, views and perspectives are often different when returning. With only a couple hundred feet of elevation change, the return trip is not difficult; the most challenging climb is the one out of the Snow Hole itself. ⚹

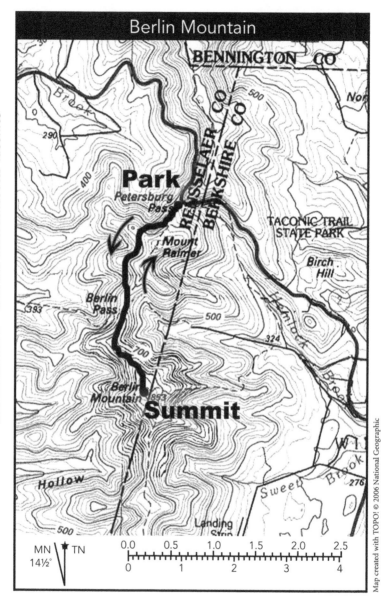

Berlin Mountain

Highlight: View from the summit

Hike Length: 5.5 miles round trip
Hike Difficulty: Easy to moderate
Starting Elevation: 2,080'
Highest Elevation: 2,818'

Directions:

MA/NY 2 to Petersburg Pass, which is .2 miles west of the state border. Parking is on the south side of the road.

GPS

Parking:	42°43.39; 73°16.67
Summit:	42°41.52; 73°17.15

The Taconic Mountains straddle the New York-Massachusetts border for its entire length. One result of this geographic separation is a lack of identity and continuity in the eyes of people and establishments. When looking at the political boundaries of either state, the impression made by the Taconics is far less than when seen as a whole. Spilling into Connecticut and attaining their greatest heights in Vermont, the Taconics' identity is further divided. Few organizations or agencies treat the mountains as a continuous body, making the understanding of the region's natural history more difficult. As a result, many places are poorly known or inaccurately represented in a regional context.

Berlin Mountain is a prime example of this mountain chain's loss of geographic integrity. Rising to 2,818 feet above sea level, it is the highest point in the New York State section of the Taconic Mountains, and the highest point in the state not in the Adirondacks or Catskills.

Despite this, Berlin Mountain lives in relative obscurity, part of a mountain ridge that wanders in and out of Massachusetts. Moreover, Mount Greylock's additional 550 feet across the Green River Valley dwarfs Berlin's summit. The state line is only about 200 feet east of Berlin's summit, and the elevation here is more than 200 feet higher than Mount Everett, which is often thought of (incorrectly) as the second-highest peak in the Massachusetts Taconics.

The trail to Berlin Mountain begins at the Petersburg Pass, just west of the New York-Massachusetts line. The entire hike follows the Taconic Crest Trail, with the trail escaping the parking area at its southwest corner. The parking area abuts the extinct Petersburg Pass ski area; the fossilized ski trails are slowly being reclaimed by the mixed hardwood forest. The ski area carved the slopes of 2,575-foot Mount Raimer, the first major landmark between the pass and Berlin Mountain. After a few steps along the wide, level path, the trail reaches an open view to the northwest, which includes White Rocks, the town of Petersburg, and the Hoosic River Valley. Many lower hills, outcrops formed of Taconic strata, pepper the landscape. To the west is a lower Taconic ridgeline.

The area is full of well-established side trails and old logging roads, making the route hard to follow at times; however, the blue markers of the NYSDEC and the white diamonds of the Taconic Crest Trail eliminate the confusion. The rock here is typical of the Taconics—flaky, shiny green and gray layers, folded and bent into all sorts of contorted forms. This rock is not all that erosion-resistant, meaning the Taconic Range here is decaying faster than some of the surrounding mountain regions. As compensation, the eroding rocks produce greater amounts of nutrient-filled soils, giving the local vegetation more resources than on other mountain masses. Alder, birch and oak colonize the trailside area, the thousands upon thousands of thin tree stems a testament to the slope's open conditions not long ago. Club moss and woodland fern are common forest-floor residents. As the trail heads south, American beech join the forest, and a few of the trees are larger, telling of longer uninterrupted growth and recovery times for the forest. In early spring this area is rich with spring beauties, trout lilies, red trillium and yellow violets. Piliated woodpeckers glide between the larger trees searching for ants, beetles, fruits and nuts. Sometimes their percussions echo through the air.

Skirting Mount Raimer affords the chance to warm up before the trail takes on a much steeper slope on the way to crossing Raimer's western shoulder. Covered in fine gravel and studded with layer after layer of Taconic schist, the trail works its way up and over the mountain. The trail is heavily eroded, and no section of the trail to Berlin Mountain is more demanding. To the north, the steep slope affords a good view, with the bumps and lumps of Taconics stretching into Vermont. The path then levels off along the mountain ridge, where a few hemlock, red spruce and sugar maple join the forest. Forest diversity is high, with the Taconics' metamorphic rock decaying into relatively fertile soils for the upper elevations of a mountain range. When combined with the poor drainage crafted by the recent ice age, wet and muddy ground becomes an additional trail challenge.

As soon as the trail begins to head down Mount Raimer and gains a southern exposure, the forest reflects the warmer conditions. Oak and birch dominate. Grasses coat the ground. Forest diversity decreases as the sun dries and heats south-facing slopes quickly. In places the oaks and birches spread out in a sea of grasses, the forest appearing more like a cultivated orchard than a wild landscape. Unfortunately, the direct sunshine cannot dry out the muddy trail and its deep, ATV-enhanced puddles. Staying out of the mud and deep water is challenging, and each foray into the surrounding vegetation increases the size of the damaged areas.

As the trail continues its downhill course, the land falls away before it, revealing a splendid view of Berlin Pass and Berlin Mountain to the south and the northern and eastern fronts of the Catskills in the distance. Berlin Mountain wears a thin veneer of red spruce around its summit. On all but the clearest days, the Catskills are shrouded in a man-inspired gray-brown haze. Mount Greylock's mass rises to the east, its presence a reminder that the Taconics offer much higher peaks than Berlin and Raimer. Since the trail generally follows the high ridge, its ascension of Berlin Mountain is easy to pick out. The gray muddy mess filling much of Berlin Pass is an ominous sign of more wet terrain to come

The drop into Berlin Pass is direct. The ground is rocky, the schists often slippery. The forest is sparse and the open, south-facing slope heats up quickly on sunny days, keeping the land dry and the vegetation less diverse; however, the blueberries are spectacular and in August produce a bumper crop of tasty treats. Winds often howl through the pass and up the open slopes.

As soon as the trail climbs out of the pass, the sheltering slopes of Berlin Mountain provide better growing conditions. The air cools, and a lush forest of birch, hemlock, oak and spruce covers the mountain. Wildflowers and ground cover are more plentiful as well. As in the pass, land ownership is fragmented, with New York State's yellow boundary markers often near or crossing the Taconic Crest Trail.

The climb up Berlin Mountain is long, but only moderately steep. Once the ridge rises above the pass, the land begins to fall away to either side, giving the trail an Alpine feel. The forest is inviting, filled with warm greens, golds and browns. Water is more plentiful once off the exposed slopes, and the trail often doubles as a small streambed. Quite clear, the water makes the eroded trail and rock even more slippery. Alongside the trail, beech rejoins the forest, its smooth silvery-gray bark appearing more sophisticated among the rougher bark of adjoining species. On approaching the mountain's rounded summit, the trees become stunted. Soon, spruce join the

*Mount Greylock, Massachusetts' highest point, is clearly visible from
Berlin Mountain, New York's highest peak not in the Adirondacks or
Catskills.*

forest in larger numbers. The thick healthy growth of spruce greets hikers like a high-elevation ambassador. Unfortunately, there is not much of a spruce-clad country here, as the trail quickly passes through the dense, dark evergreens and emerges onto a wide dome of low-cut grass. The mountain's even curvature reveals a little more of the surrounding scene with each step. Step one and there is nothing on the horizon. Step two and Greylock blasts into the scene. Step three and wow—the surrounding Taconics appear along the southern view. Step four and in come the Catskills to the southwest.

Once at the top, the view extends in all directions, with only a few of the taller spruce blocking some of the vista. The entire summit is open and forms a gentle dome. A few concrete blocks make an informal memorial to a long-gone fire tower, but the treeless mountaintop needs no tower to display its outstanding views. To the west rise Albany's towers. To the east is Greylock's lighthouse. To the northeast are the Green Mountains and their Massachusetts offspring, the Hoosac Range. A look north extends back toward Mount Equinox, highest point in the Taconics. The view is one of the most striking in the range, the mountain's open dome a great viewing platform.

The hike back is a reverse route of the ascent, but this time the hardest part of the journey is the climb out of Berlin Pass onto Mount Raimer. The return also allows for a better perspective of the Taconic Range to the north as the mountains travel into Vermont toward their highest summits. ⚹

• 2 •

Vermont's Champion
Taconic Mountains

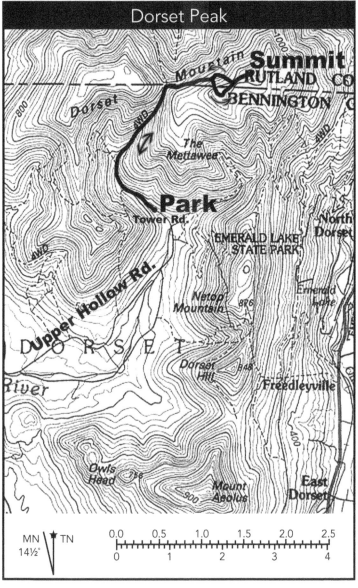

Vermont's Champion Taconic Mountains

66

MN / TN
14½°

0.0   0.5   1.0   1.5   2.0   2.5

0   1   2   3   4

Map created with TOPO! © 2006 National Geographic

Dorset Peak

Highlights: The highest wild spot in the Taconics
Hike Length: 6.4 miles round trip
Hike Difficulty: Moderate to strenuous
Starting Elevation: 1,460'
Highest Elevation: 3,770'

Directions:

VT Route 30 to Dorset Hollow Rd. (north) for .8 miles.
Right on Upper Rd. for 2 miles. The road continues as
Tower Rd. for about a half mile to parking area.

GPS:

Parking (Dunbar Rd.):	43°17.06; 73°02.82
Southwest Summit:	43°18.32; 73°02.18
Northeast Summit:	43°18.53; 73°01.70

Dorset Peak is the northernmost high peak in the Taconic Range. At 3,770 feet it also pokes its way into the 100 highest peaks of New England as number 99 (only New Hampshire's northeasternmost Cannon Ball is lower within this northeastern mountain clique). Within the Taconics, however, Dorset clearly takes the silver medal for Taconic Mountain heights. And with its higher brother, Equinox, tamed by a road and many creature comforts, Dorset Peak's isolated and wild forests make for the Taconics' highest wild place.

Like much of mountain geography, understanding the layout of Dorset Mountain and its summits can be tricky. Dorset Mountain is much more than Dorset Peak; it includes the 3,400-foot Jackson Peak to the west. Dorset Peak itself has two summits; the southwestern peak is about forty feet lower than the 3,770-foot northeastern peak. The southwestern peak has the remains of a fire tower and provides a limited, yet attractive view to the northwest. The higher, northeastern peak sports the ruins of an old cabin, but is hemmed in by a thick conifer and birch forest.

Dorset Peak can be reached using a variety of routes, but with its complex network of poorly marked old logging roads and snowmobile trails, the approach from the south via Dorset Hollow is the best choice. It is direct and steep, but well-surfaced. Overall the trail is hard on the legs and easy on the feet. A look up the hollow at Jackson Peak's imposing evergreen-capped heights easily confirms—and even underestimates—the upcoming challenge.

The trail begins as a rough road/trail hybrid at the end of Tower Road. Jane Brook escorts the road and remains a constant companion into the saddle between Dorset Peak and Jackson Peak. The stream's frothy roar fills the air of the cool, often shaded, hollow. Mountain walls close in from the west, north and east. Using the stream's previous work to grade the land, the route climbs slowly through a forest of birch, maple and beech. Most of the trees are young, but in some places the second-growth trees are tall and straight. Small, cleared fields also adjoin the trail, the tall grasses a reminder of decades past when the mountain's lower slopes were cleared for logging or agriculture.

In a few places the trail crosses the stream. After a heavy rain or in the spring, this crossing can be tricky, especially to those without waterproof shoes. Once past an old cabin, the land begins to climb sharply, the shrinking stream becoming a ribbon of noisy whitewater. Often wet, footing can be tough and the trail muddy. The forest continues to sport its young collection of beech, maple and birch, but white birch becomes more prominent as the climb continues. On the sheltered slopes, spruce and fir begin to appear in increasing numbers. A look upslope shows that the trend will continue.

Descending quickly from the mountain slopes, the feeder streams building Jane Brook can trace their history to the end of the ice age. When the continental glacier retreated, it left behind a veneer of till. Finding the fastest way down through the point of least resistance, the steep stream courses used waterpower to remove the till. In turn, this created the stream's small, steep, V-shaped valleys. Without too much water or too much till to remove, these V-shaped valleys are relatively small. In contrast, note the U-shaped, rounded forms of the mountain peaks—all are landforms crafted by massive sheets of solid ice, not running water.

After a tough constant climb, the trail begins to level as it approaches the gap between the higher peaks. Conifers come to dominate the forest, their fresh smell and dark green needles a boreal introduction to Dorset's higher elevations. The mountain slopes close in tight, the steep, simple lines of the Taconics' higher elevations revealed firsthand. Upon leveling off, the saddle continues to tease the hiker, drawing the route to the northern edge of Dorset before capping the actual saddle and reaching a trail junction.

Among the more enclosed saddles in the Taconics, this is one of the easiest places to envision why such gaps often become wind tunnels. On approaching the saddle, the wind often increases. First the treetops begin to sway, and the rushing air sings through the leaves, needles and branches. Soon the breeze reaches the ground, often welcome in the summer and a bane in the winter. So, why all the wind here? The answer, literally, lies in the land. The sharp notch and the lack of earth allow air to flow over the mountain here. First, it is important to note that air behaves a lot like water, even if people cannot see it. The notch is the first point where air can flow over Dorset Mountain. Thus, the air, as it wants to spill over the mountain, gets its first chance to flow here. The moving air is the wind. As the lowest place where the air can flow, a lot of air tries to move through this spot, again increasing the local winds.

Dorset Mountain, the second-highest Taconic peak, offers only a limited view to the north that provides a good overview of the northernmost Taconics.

After the saddle junction, the trail turns right, heading northeast. The trail is not steep and continues through a forest more and more dominated by spruce and fir. The thick foliage and northern slope keep the route dark and cool. The sun only provides a glancing blow of light and warmth. A few side trails head off to the left. After less than a half mile, another snowmobile trail, occasionally marked with silver squares, steeply heads to the right. The climbing is hard, but not as taxing as the steep slopes leading into the saddle. The bright trunks of paper birch stand out among the sea of green and brown. After a little more than a quarter mile, the snowmobile trail reaches a junction with a steep foot trail. A quick jaunt up the steep slope delivers the trail to Dorset Peak's southwestern summit.

Reaching the summit does not bring thoughts of isolation and wild places. The rusting remains of a steel fire tower, the lowest level inviting but dangerous-looking at the same time, greet visitors. The trail cut provides a limited view to the northwest, where a few lines of lower Taconic summits, most notably 2,800-foot Tinmouth Mountain and 2,400-foot Dutch Hill, gather east of the valley. Beyond them stands the last true sentinel of the Taconics—2,726-foot Herrick Mountain, which rises southwest of Rutland. Farther west, a bumpy set of lower hills and ridges gathers just east of the New York–Vermont border. Farms, lakes and wetlands fill the Tinmouth Valley. A slightly improved version of this view was available at one time from the tower, but climbing the now-rickety structure is not a recommended activity. The shaky remains are not high enough to reveal a panoramic view, but they are more than adequate to degrade the fir-crowned summit's aesthetics.

From this lower, showier summit, the trail continues to the east for a half mile, descending into a small gap and then climbing to the mountain's true summit. The trail, sparsely marked with orange triangles, drops into a small saddle thick with spruce and fir. In the small depression, a trail junction marks the route before the path climbs

Dorset's higher, northeastern peak. The climb is not taxing, and once heading uphill, trail conditions improve.

The forest remains the domain of spruce and fir, taking on the characteristics of this boreal, high-elevation forest. The soil is dark and organic, the mineral component stripped away by glaciers and rain. Drainage is poor. When dry, footing is soft and comfortable, but when wet, deep puddles of water and muck make each step range from annoying to miserable. Needles hang over the trail and protrude from the trail's sides, encasing the path in a tunnel of dark vegetation. Any detour becomes not merely unwise but impractical as well.

Dorset's true summit is heavily clad in a spruce-fir forest. A sign-in canister and a decaying log structure adorn the summit. Compared to the more open southwestern peak, there is little reason to linger here.

A return to the saddle along the orange-marked path delivers the trail to a junction. A turn to the right (north) begins a steady descent. Dorset Mountain does not have many variations in its topography, allowing resident trails to maintain long straight stretches. After a long descent, the trail merges with the lower snowmobile trail, which continues downhill, eventually rejoining the route used to climb Dorset's southwestern summit. From this point the trail follows the path used to ascend the mountain.

Winter brings a whole new dimension to this hike. Although not teeming with wildlife, snow reveals tracks of snowshoe hares, deer, grouse and mice. Many of the ground features hide beneath the uniform snowy blanket. The land becomes brighter and colder, with the snow's brilliance dominating even the sky on cloudy days. Ice and snow collect on the masses of evergreen needles, weighing down the trees and creating winter highlights. On sunny days, these snow- and ice-encrusted trees paint the forest with the light of a million diamonds and a million rainbows. ⚡

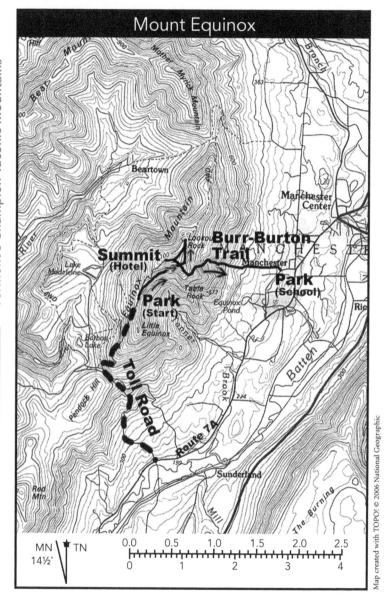

74

Mount Equinox

Highlights: Extensive views, impressive cirques
Hike Length: 4.4 miles one way
Hike Difficulty: Moderate
Starting Elevation: 3,150'
Highest Elevation: 3,848'

Directions:

VT 7A (Main St., Ethan Allen Highway), about 3.2 miles south of West St. in Manchester. Turn on Skyline Dr. (west side of road, pay toll). Follow Skyline Dr. about 4.9 miles to saddle between Equinox and Little Equinox. Park along road. Trailhead on right.

GPS

Parking (Skyline Drive):	43°09.30; 73°07.63
Lookout Rock:	43°10.22; 73°06.67
Summit:	43°09.95; 73°07.03
Parking (Manchester Center):	43°09.61; 73°05.03

Equinox is an enigma when it comes to exploration. A toll road offers an easy route to the top, yet this energy-inefficient choice detracts from the intimacy needed to really appreciate the mountaintop. On the other hand there is a steep, direct trail to the top, which rises more than 2,800 feet in just over two miles. Unfortunately, the Burr-Burton Trail offers few perks besides grueling exercise and the reality that, once near the top, a paved road, a parking lot, an aging hotel, antennas galore and many people greet the weary solace-seeker.

Thus, the tallest mountain in one of the most underappreciated mountain chains in the nation presents a dilemma—what route to use to get to the top? First, it is important to note that ascending the mountain is important for two reasons: it is the Taconics' highest point, and the mountaintop unveils views among the most extensive and impressive in the Northeast.

A small network of trails winds around the summit, but they are poorly marked and, for the most part, little used. A crude map of the summit trails is available, but it is almost as confusing as it is useful. Nonetheless, adding a little climb and a short hike to the drive returns a slice of Equinox's natural dignity, while increasing an understanding of the mountain's natural history. If two vehicles are available, then a one-way hike down the mountain is a great way to experience Equinox's stature.

The toll road is a 5.6-mile drive climbing from Route 7A south of Manchester along the southeastern face of Equinox. A few scenic overlooks add eye candy to the steep winding drive. Once atop the main ridgeline, Equinox's tamed summit comes into the view. A colony of white-clad FAA antennas grow like giant mushrooms. The Monastery Overlook, about a half mile from the top, provides the first expansive view and is a good place to begin a short exploration of the summit. To the south and west, the view is extensive, bouncing from ridge to ridge and extending into New York and Massachusetts. In the valley below lies the medieval gray stone architecture of the Carthusian Monastery and the man-made Lake Madeline. A ring of other major Taconic peaks fills the foreground, including Red Mountain, Moffitt Mountain, Bear Mountain, and Mother Myrick Mountain. Off the east side of the road, the land drops away as a precipitous cirque and tumbles into the Vermont Valley. A massive, mostly unbroken wall of Green Mountain massif stands across the valley, a sharp contrast to the Taconics' individualized peaks lining the valley's west side. Above the ridgeline soars 3,990-foot Stratton Mountain and, to the south, 3,560-foot Glastonbury Peak commands some attention as well.

A little south of the parking area, an abandoned road not open to the public climbs 3,310-foot Little Equinox. Little Equinox was once home to a wind farm and may be once again. A five-turbine wind farm would produce enough energy for about 3,500 homes. A scruffy mix of dried grasses and small trees covers Equinox's smaller peak. The peak looks inviting, but the route to the top is not accessible to the public, leaving the primary summit as the only available mountaintop destination.

The wide saddle between Little Equinox and Equinox proper provides an advantageous parking area and a natural starting point for a short hike to the summit. A loose network of trails leads to the summit, and the short walk has enough challenge and interest to make it a more natural and attractive approach.

The parking area and the initial walk along the roadside perches atop one of the Northeast's most impressive cirques. A cirque is an Alpine glacial feature carved when an isolated glacier forms or persists on steep mountain slopes. Inspired by gravity and aided by the mountainous slopes, the compacted mass of snow and ice flows downhill. As the ice tongue carves into the mountain, it scours the surface and removes soil, rock and bedrock, steepening and curving the slopes. As the small glacier flows downhill, it will typically encounter warmer conditions and begin to melt at its lower edge. Above the melting point, on the field of dirty ice, the cirque produces a wide U-shaped valley. At the margin where the ice warms and gives way to water, the running water—the start of a small stream—carves a V-shaped notch into the mountain.

Nestling into Equinox's eastern flank, the ground falls away at a rate steep enough to make a roller coaster jealous. Rarely does a road provide such access to the top of these rugged glacial landforms. A look over the side reveals Equinox's breathtaking topography and attests to the raw erosive power of an Alpine glacier. In this area a stubborn pool of mountain ice accumulated and then oozed down the mountainside as an abrasive tongue of bulldozing ice. Despite the massive rock beds supporting the mountain, the ice worked relentlessly. Inevitably, no rock can withstand the effects of Father Time. Thus, the ice gouged the mountainside and carried away the eroded material. In addition, Equinox wears another impressive cirque on its northwest face. Going back in time, it is easy to imagine an Alpine glacier lingering over and just below the summit, its lower reaches plowing into the till-filled valleys flanking the mountain.

The side trails are poorly maintained and do not receive much use, yet they offer relative isolation on what can become a very crowded mountaintop. Although the red trail is the longer route, its crossing of the cirque is uncomfortable and too close to the road to provide any isolation or sense of wilderness. The yellow trail provides a better approach to the top. This trail dives into a spruce-fir forest, along with its trappings of club moss and ferns. The spruce trees are impressive, soaring into the sky far above their birch and fir neighbors.

The yellow trail continues its march along the mountain's eastern face. The trail is not steep, but the footing is uneven and the trail is poorly marked and maintained, so the route can be confusing. If one becomes lost, most of the side trails that head uphill and to the west will lead back to the toll road. On a positive note, the sound of the cars is lost in a breezy chorus of leaves and needles. Balsam's fresh scent washes through the air. A partial view, framed by balsam fir trees, glances east across the Vermont Valley and into the Green Mountains. Then the trail continues north, passing the upper terminus of the red trail in a chaotic junction.

The yellow trail soon reaches a junction, with a crossover trail heading west and upslope to the top ridge and the toll road. The thick and ubiquitous spruce-fir forest continues to escort the trail as it traces along the cirque's upper reaches. The next trail junction comes quickly, with a small wetland marking the headwaters of a mountain stream.

Once meeting up with the blue-marked, well-maintained Burr-Burton Trail, the trail continues for another quarter mile through a thicker spruce-fire forest to an overlook called Lookout Rock. A small bench provides a flat seat at the expansive vista.

Lookout Rock peers east, overseeing almost one hundred miles of the Green Mountains from the Massachusetts border to central Vermont. Stratton Mountain's two major peaks and southern spur dominate the scene, rising far above the 2,200-foot wall creating the Green Mountains' base. The Vermont Valley slices through the foreground, creating additional elevational differences. Bromley Mountain then leads the eye along a series of Green Mountain peaks, topping off at the 4,241-foot Killington Peak. The scene can hold the eye for hours.

A rough and rutted dirt road climbs Equinox's main spine from the overlook and leads to the summit. The rocky road moves through a well-developed spruce-fir forest. A tall antenna rises near the summit, greeting the trail just before the mountaintop opens up into the grounds of the decaying Equinox Hotel. The hotel itself

Equinox is the highest Taconic peak, and its impressive views include a ring of peaks above 3,000 feet.

is an unspectacular, washed-out raised ranch constructed on a colossal scale. The uninspiring structure continues to succumb to the weather's whims. Broken siding, broken windows, cracking concrete and a general decay characterize the closed hotel.

But it is the hotel's porches that provide great views in all directions. The vista, framed by tall balsam fir trees, is fantastic. To the east is the now familiar scene stretching along the Green Mountains. To the south, west and north rise most of the remaining Taconic peaks in Vermont. Unlike the connected ridgeline of the Green Mountains, each Taconic peak rises from its own base, giving the range a more independent feel. Perhaps the most impressive view is to the west and northwest where a series of 3,000-foot peaks line the horizon. Highest among them are the twin peaks of Dorset Peak, which top off at 3,770 feet, only a few feet lower than Equinox.

Returning from Equinox provides a number of choices. Returning to the saddle is one option, but if two cars are available, leaving one at the bottom of the Burr-Burton Trail provides for a challenging downhill hike. The blue-marked Burr-Burton Trail branches off from the little-used red and yellow trails skirting Equinox's eastern face.

The red trail enters a wide dark area, the spruce-fir forest growing well on the soggy mountain shelf. The gathering stream waters finally start to have an impact on the steep land, adding its growing V-shaped valley to the glacially smoothed slopes. In this geologic interchange, the blue-marked Burr-Burton Trail begins its crazy descent. Over its steepest 1.1 miles, the trail descends 2,100 feet, more than double the grade of what typically constitutes a steep trail.

The trail does not wander. Club moss, birch, spruce and fir line the mountainside. White rock, quartz, is prevalent among the metamorphosed rock masses. Together, the white quartz combines with the white trunks of paper birch to stripe the mountains with hints of the snow and ice that winter brings to this mighty summit. The trail makes a bend toward Manchester Center and, hitting the nebulous summit edge, significantly increases in steepness. Through the curtain of trees, needles and leaves, hints of views across the Vermont Valley appear, but never materialize. In late summer, the hobblebush leaves serve as advance guard for fall color, bringing their brick-red and purple tones to the otherwise green forest.

Once below the realm of the spruce-fir forest, a maple-birch community becomes the dominant forest cover. Hobblebush and mountain maple are common in the understory. A dark accent of red spruce continues to give the forest a darker edge. Individual spruce trees grow to impressive stature. Before the timber industry harvested much of the region's larger spruce growth, red spruce gave much of the mountains a more boreal appearance. Red spruce was a preferred wood for airplanes, musical instruments and paper.

The trail moves along mountain slopes that are among the Taconics' most aggressive—this is another part of the cirque defining Equinox's shape. Although not as impressive or well defined as the cirques on the southeastern and northwestern mountain faces, this cirque is easy to identify on a topographic map.

With the trail retaining a straight orientation, it is not surprising the route eroded deeply into the landscape. Water flowing down the long unbroken stretches has little to slow its progress, and it carries generous amounts of Equinox away with it. As a result, large rocks and steep banks characterize the trail.

As the path progresses down the mountain, yellow birch becomes a dominant part of the forest community. Armies of yellow birch saplings line the mountainside like raw recruits training in the ways of the forest. With their bronze sheen, the forest takes on an almost metallic glow as the masses of slender, straight trees stand at attention.

Slightly south (right) of the trail, a short spur leads to a gushing spring. An honor guard of yellow birch in their copper dress uniforms lines the trail. Surrounding the site is an impressive stand of jewelweed, which thrives in the moist conditions. The water, flowing underground above this point, surges from the mountainside, appearing overjoyed at reaching the surface after days, years, or perhaps even centuries spent as groundwater. A large-diameter PVC pipe tames the newborn stream's natural enthusiasm, but the blast of cold, fresh water looks, sounds and feels impressive. The water is frigid; it is a challenge to keep a hand in the water for more than a few seconds. A water filter makes this fresh flow potable and is a definite extra bonus. Below the spring, the water immediately becomes a significant surface stream sliding its way down the steep mountainside even faster than the steep trail.

The trail provides one last glimpse of the Vermont Valley before becoming more recognizable as an old road and slowing its rate of descent. Knees, ankles and quadriceps all can take a collective sigh. The forest benefits from the moderating slopes as well. Here, the mature trees are very large, healthy and stable, despite the relatively shallow soils and steep slopes. The forest continues becoming more northern hardwood in character—maple, beech and birch, with hemlock lining the streams. The understory disappears and a healthy, mature second-growth forest covers the mountainside. The Taconic Mountains, with their varied rock types and calcareous basement rock, are more fertile than their Green Mountain neighbors.

To complete the journey to Manchester Center, the Burr-Burton Trail intersects a network of formal and informal trails as it enters a heavily visited recreation area. The main trail widens, and improved engineering works the trail into the mountain's contours. Soon the old road becomes more serviceable and flattens. In the surrounding forest, oaks join with the dominant northern hardwoods. Thick spreads of maidenhair fern and wild asters escort weary legs to the parking area along Manchester Center's upper flank. ⚹

• 3 •

The Southern Taconics
and Berkshires

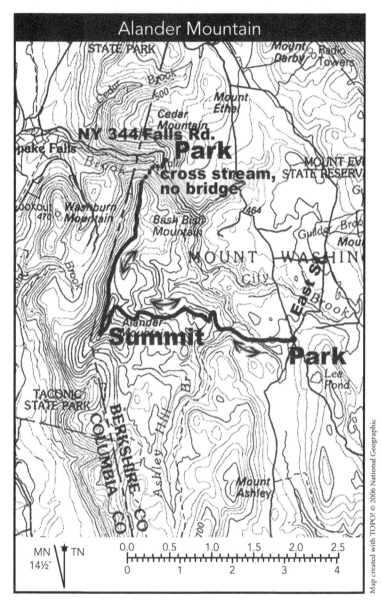

Alander Mountain

The Southern Taconics and Berkshires

84

Map created with TOPO! © 2006 National Geographic

Alander Mountain

Highlight: Views from the summit

Via Bash Bish:

> **Hike Length:** 5.6 miles
> **Hike Difficulty:** Moderate to strenuous
> **Starting Elevation:** 1,245'
> **Highest Elevation:** 2,235'

Via East St.:

> **Hike Length:** 5.0 miles
> **Hike Difficulty:** Moderate
> **Starting Elevation:** 1,655'
> **Highest Elevation:** 2,235'

Directions:

Via Bash Bish:

NY 344 to MA border. Road becomes Falls Rd. Continue uphill (east) for about .5 miles to parking area on right. Note: There is an additional parking area for the falls in New York along Route 344.

Via East Street:

MA Route 41 (just south of junction with MA 23) to Mt. Washington Rd. (west side of road). Follow Mt. Washington Rd. for about 3 miles to where it becomes East St. Follow East St. for about 4.5 miles to junction with West St. Parking area on right (west side of road), part of the state forest complex.

GPS

Parking (upper Bash Bish):	42°06.90; 73°29.49
Parking (East Street):	42°05.18; 73°27.73
Summit:	42°05.28; 73°30.26

Alander Mountain is not a summit that draws the eye from surrounding landscapes. When looking at the western Taconics, Alander Mountain does not even stand out among its neighbors. Even from close vantages, its gentle rounded summit blends into the somewhat deceiving pastoral charm of the southern Taconics. Like many of the surrounding peaks, Alander's summit presents a rocky accent atop its gentle rounded mass, complete with a craggy hint of the Scottish Highlands.

Set on the New York–Massachusetts border, Alander's 2,235-foot summit tops off a few hundred feet east of the Empire State. Where the mountain's southwestern shoulder reaches the state line, at 2,110-feet, it marks Columbia County's highest point. Alander Mountain presents two reasonable approaches, although one of the trails requires a tricky, a.k.a. wet, crossing of Bash Bish Creek. During periods of high water or cold weather, fording the stream can be dangerous and is not recommended. Still, each approach provides a different and enjoyable hike to Alander and its expansive views. Both trails require driving into the wild, rugged, and almost forgotten corner of southwestern Massachusetts.

Alander Mountain has two options when approached from the north, each with a trade-off. The longer route begins along NY Route 344 in the parking area for Bash Bish Falls. This taxing route takes a little over a mile to ascend Bash Bish Mountain's lower slopes. Then the trail joins the shorter, but equally steep, quarter-mile trail from the upper parking area along Bash Bish Creek. A gravel road leads from the upper parking area to the stream, and the challenge lies in finding a reasonable stream crossing. The water is swift, cold and at least knee-deep. Only during a dry season is the crossing likely to be easy. Soaked socks and hiking shoes five minutes into the adventure do not always make for an enjoyable hike.

Before beginning the walk to the stream, the steep landscape provides a visual bonus. A short scramble up the rocks at the upper parking area's southwestern corner leads to a spectacular vista to the west. Spilling out of the steep clove, the view crosses bumpy lines of Taconic Hills, the sunken Hudson Valley and eastern Catskills. Even though the Catskills are thirty miles away, their summits present an impressive western horizon. Popular hiking destinations themselves, hikers in the eastern Catskills often stop to appreciate the view to the east that includes Alander Mountain and the Bash Bish Valley.

Once on the route to Alander, the wide gravel path wanders down to the Bash Bish Creek's clear, energetic waters. Without a bridge or ford, the moderately wide stream is a challenge to cross without getting wet. There really is no best route, since each small flood reworks the stream course. Having a pair of knee-high boots for the crossing eliminates a potentially soggy trek up the Taconics' western face. By leaving the boots behind for the return crossing, the challenging wade across becomes less of a concern. With waterfalls nearby, however, it is best to skip this crossing and choose another approach to Alander when the water is too high.

On the creek's southern side, a blue-marked trail up Bash Bish Mountain begins as a series of informal paths that collect near the steep fence line. The fence protects people, as well as the delicate and treacherous environment around Bash Bish Falls, from each other. The climb up the mountain is extremely steep. The roar and echoes of the rushing water is impressive. Dark hemlocks shade the north-facing slopes. Down the valley, a sheer drop of 300 feet provides a look and feel more akin to the grandeur of the Rocky Mountains. Along the chasm's northern face rises the 1,870-foot Cedar Mountain.

The blue trail formally begins at the top of the steepest part of the cliff. The markings appear seemingly out of nowhere. Lower on the mountain, the route is often confusing, and only higher up do the bold blue blazes appear. Blackberries and white wood asters are common on the forest floor. The climb remains extremely steep, and footing can be difficult. The trail continues at a calf-burning pace. After completing the strenuous climb, the blue trail merges into the white-marked Taconic Crest Trail.

Soon after joining the Taconic Crest Trail, the path continues to lift on Bash Bish Mountain's building slopes. Transitioning from the moist environment along the clove and stream, hemlocks go from playing a dominant role to a supporting one. The canopy opens a bit and some light filters through to the forest floor and its thicker understory. The trail soon hits the mountain's top ridge and turns toward Alander. Red maple, pitch pine, scrub oak, mountain laurel, blueberry and blackberry cover the summit—a typical vegetation spread for the Taconics. In places the scrappy forest parts just enough to reveal occasional glimpses of the Catskills.

The northeastern view from Alander Mountain includes Mount Everett and Race Mountain.

The trail remains level and generally straight along the ridge for a long stretch as it heads for Alander. A few small viewpoints continue to peer to the west, but none are impressive enough for more than a quick glance. Then, a break in the forest ahead and a small dip accent Alander's 300-foot rise as it makes a surprising entrance. Although not imposing, the climb is significant and a welcome break from the easy ridge walk over from Bash Bish Mountain. The trail meets up with the Alander Mountain Trail near the summit, but the mountain's vistas begin well before the trail junction.

🚶 🚶 🚶

For those not wishing to cross a rushing stream in which getting soaked up to the knee is the rule, the best route to Alander is from the heart of Mount Washington township. The trail begins next to the Mount Washington State Forest headquarters, nestled within the rugged Bash Bish Creek watershed, one of the state's most isolated valleys. Thick, lush forest lines the small, rough roads, making the broken pavement more of a hint of a wide trail, rather than an actual thoroughfare for cars.

The hike to Alander begins by moving through a mix of rolling fields and scattered woodlands. Mountain breezes form wavy patterns among the grass. South of the trail, Hunt Pond's calm waters glisten beyond the fields. The dark waters appear foreboding against the verdant fields and bright sky. Stories of mythical mountain beasts living within the dark waters would feel appropriate here. Surrounding the valley, soft, rounded mountain shapes poke above the tree line. Overall, the impression is of an isolated, yet comfortable landscape, with only a hint or two of wild places.

As a blend of field and forest, the route's first quarter mile is a haven for wildflowers and birds. From early spring through late fall, this area sports colorful accents representing every shade of the rainbow.

On a musical note, birdsong fills the air with a symphony of sound. Keep an eye and ear peeled for red-eyed vireos, American goldfinches and hermit thrushes. The forests lining the fields are young and unorganized, as pioneer species now dominate these once open fields. Sprouting in what were farms only a few decades ago are paper birch, white pine and red maple, but they share the forest census with a variety of additional species.

The trail mainly heads downhill and soon offers the first view of Alander. The mountain appears as a challenging, if not imposing, peak. Then the trail leaves the open fields and heads into a young forest. Headwaters racing toward Bash Bish Creek escort the trail into darker woods. Hemlocks line the stream, and a northern hardwood forest—mainly birch, beech and maple—dominates the hilly terrain. The cold stream waters act as a natural air conditioner and humidifier, cooling and moistening the air, helping the hemlocks to win out over other, competitive species.

The trail continues its downhill course, following the tone set by the declining stream. Soon the trail passes signs for a campground before reaching a larger stream valley. The elevated trail reveals a good view into the forest as it climbs and the stream decreases in elevation. Yellow birch, hemlock, sugar maple and striped maple are the most common trees, with dark hemlocks shading the area around the stream. Along the trail, the flowing plastic look of the local metamorphic rock draws the eyes, while in the distance, the high slopes on the stream's far side rise upon these same rock types.

No longer able to approach the mountain and still remain near stream valleys, the trail steepens and the land takes on a more mountainous character. Soils become shallow and large rocks pepper the ground. Ferns line and brighten the understory. Indian pipes are common. Bereft of thick ground cover, the trail provides a good view into the forest canopy. Cherry, birch and maple dominate the forest.

On a small crest, the trail passes a major landmark—a sign indicating a campground that lies down the spur trail branching off to the south (left). Away from the stream and working steadily uphill, a drier forest community begins to predominate. As water availability decreases, fire risk and fire-adjusted species increase. Perhaps most noticeable is the prevalence of mountain laurel. In late June, its waxy, light pink and white flowers explode like natural fireworks. Chestnut oak, northern red oak and paper birch join the forest.

Keeping a moderate uphill track, the trail becomes more challenging. Rough rocks and small boulders interrupt the till-covered ground. Alongside the trail, coral mushrooms and club mosses decorate the mountainside. Slender young trees dominate the forest, yet there are few understory trees—leaving this forest without a replacement cohort. Instead, the dense stands of mountain laurel monopolize the ground cover. Without a new set of seedlings and saplings, this area could evolve into a "laurel bald," where only the dense, almost impenetrable stems of this scrub cover the mountainside. Although beautiful in June when its pink blossoms erupt, these monocultures are unwelcoming to most wildlife and limit local biological diversity.

The trail becomes more rugged as the elevation accumulates. Bright white quartz chips and veins, signs of the area's metamorphic past, coat the mountain. The darker slates and schists are the metamorphic products of shales deposited in ancient seas long ago.

After working its way to the east side of the mountain, the trail passes a small cabin. Near the cabin, the trail meets up with the white-marked Taconic Crest Trail. The trail turns right (west) and begins to climb the outcrops and boulders topping Alander. The vegetation remains dominated by oaks, but tree height falls as the weather takes its toll on the exposed slopes. The climb is steep, but short. Soon the trail reaches the crest and views open up in both directions, with a short trip to the south and north worth the effort.

At the Summit

Among the many spectacular viewpoints along Alander Mountain's crest, perhaps the most impressive are those from its north face. With many layers of ridges and valleys, along with numerous summits in view, the area takes on a deeper dimension of mountainous character. To the west are a series of 3,500-foot peaks, the Catskill Mountains' eastern escarpment. To the north the ridgeline carries off toward Bash Bish and Cedar mountains. To the east the land rises again, capping off along the summits of Mount Race and the 2,602-foot Mount Everett.

Like many of the Taconic peaks, a rock cairn adorns the summit. The open mountaintop, with its rocky template and grassy fields, is reminiscent of the Scottish Highlands. There are many spots where views are spectacular, with many worth the time to stop for lunch or pictures. To the west, in addition to the Hudson Valley and the Catskills, Stissing Mountain in Dutchess County is in view. To the east, neighboring Ashley Hill, Mount Frisell and Brace Mountain sculpt the horizon.

Alander Mountain is a great hike via either route, but the varieties of the landscape and the differences in the approaches make a strong argument for trying both. With the starting points for each hike only about ten miles apart, a circuit hike is a great option if two cars are available. On the way back the steep slopes and stream crossing are tricky obstacles, but care and caution will carry the day. As a bonus, the stream crossing on the return is so close to the parking area that wet feet are not as much of a concern. ⚹

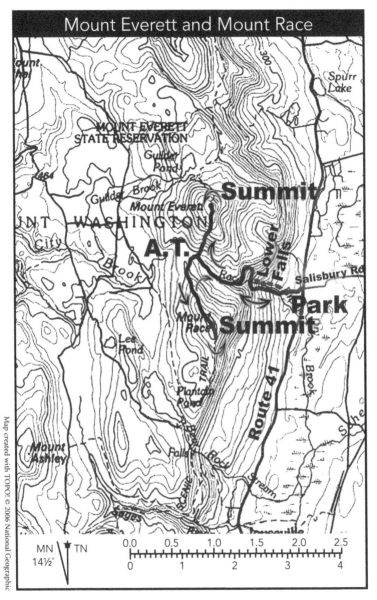

Mount Everett and Mount Race

Highlight: View from Mount Race

Hike Length: 7.2 miles round trip
Hike Difficulty: Moderate to strenuous
Starting Elevation: 750'
Highest Elevation: 2,602'

Directions:

MA 41 to 2.5 miles north of CT border (or 1.5 miles south of Berkshire School Rd.) Parking is on west, across from Salisbury Rd.

GPS

Parking:	42°05.37; 73°24.67
Everett Summit:	42°06.12; 73°25.94
Race Summit:	42°04.93; 73°25.90

Mount Everett and Mount Race are best hiked as a duo. With both peaks accessed by the steep and taxing two-mile trail paralleling Race Brook, the hike in to the notch between the two mountains makes visiting both peaks a wise investment. Each mountain offers different highlights, yet both are grand destinations. At 2,602 feet, Mount Everett is the highest peak in the southern Taconics and the southernmost point in New England above 2,500 feet. A regional landmark, the peak is easily identified rising above its neighbors from fifty and more miles away. Landscape painters of the mid-1800s recognized Everett's looming presence, highlighting it in pieces such as Wenzler's *A View of Great Barrington*. Everett also sports a decent view of the Catskills, from where Mount Everett stands out as the most prominent landform along the eastern horizon. Mount Race simply displays one of the region's finest vistas. If a choice between the two peaks must come to pass—if time is short or legs are tired—Mount Race provides the easier and more impressive destination.

The most advantageous climb up to these neighboring peaks begins along Race Brook, the stream separating Everett from Race. Race Brook is a jumpy, aggressive and frothy stream. Its series of waterfalls, usually referred to as five falls, but impossible to fully separate, is a worthy destination in its own right. Along its steepest mile, the stream gains slightly more than 1,000 feet—among the steepest watercourses in the eastern United States. From the trail as it first encounters the waterfalls, a look upstream reveals a sharp, V-shaped, water-carved valley within the wide, U-shaped, glacier-carved clove.

The first section of trail is unspectacular, heading over an intermittent stream before cutting through open fields and a second-growth oak and laurel forest. The blue-marked trail splits, with the main trail heading (left) south, while an older trail continues (straight) west to the bottom of lower Race Brook Falls. Faint red-paint blazes unreliably mark the old trail as it parallels Race Brook's northern bank. To return to the main trail from the bottom of the first falls requires either climbing up the southern bank's slippery, steep and unstable slopes or backtracking.

Beyond the junction, the blue trail crosses Race Brook and the route works its way along the southern bank. The water is exceptionally clear with hues of green, gray and gold glittering in the water. After crossing the stream, the trail ascends quickly while Race Brook remains at the slender valley floor, having already completed the bulk of its downward journey. In the gorge, hemlock dominates the forest, the cool, moist and sheltered environment favoring this evergreen species. For a time the trail heads away from the stream, skirting the edge of the hemlock forest along a brighter, drier, oak forest. The stream takes a more direct course, the silence growing as the playful waters fade into the background. Soon the stream will plunge down Race Brook Falls, and like many great performers, it needs some time backstage to prepare.

By the time a sign reveals a side path to the falls, the trail is already higher than the first fall, so the spur trail heads downhill. Heavily shaded by the hemlocks, the cool waters fill the sharp valley with natural air conditioning. The falls begin to show through the trees. The trail leads to a couple of awkward views of a spectacular falls, but the dangerous terrain requires caution. At this point an older trail, no longer marked nor maintained, continues up along the stream but is hard to follow. Returning along the spur trail to the blue-marked trail is longer, but less steep and less confusing.

While the new trail avoids the sensitive and dangerous terrain along the stream by skirting the gorge's southern side, the older trail heads up along Race Brook Falls, dancing alongside the vibrant water. Every couple of steps introduces new falls and cascades. The cool damp air around the fall encourages slick, mossy surfaces. Energy is a constant theme here. Although none of the additional falls along this route are as impressive as the lower falls, and most of the drops are more cascade than free-fall, the rock and water remain spectacular. Only the fall just above the junction of the stream and the blue-marked trail compares in height and breadth with the lower fall.

The two routes converge at this second high waterfall. Heading north, the trail crosses the stream and heads uphill and away from the

The views from Mount Race are among the best in the Taconics.

water. On these south-facing slopes, the hemlocks disappear, with oak, maple and beech coming into the forest. A drier landscape dominates, and mountain laurel and witch hazel grow along the trail. Although less steep, the hike remains challenging.

After rounding a sharp bend, the trail levels off and again heads south. White pine and blueberries round out the flora. A quaint view to the east and southeast looks upon the Litchfield Hills and southern Berkshires, with the hills topping off in the 1,800 to 2,000-foot range. A shoulder of Mount Everett is also visible to the north, a not-so-subtle reminder of the awaiting climb. In this area white oak—a species not typically found above the valleys—persists.

Rushing water reintroduces the trail to Race Brook, and shady hemlocks once again dominate the forest. A coolness lost on the less humid, more exposed ridge returns to the air. Now above the steep gorge and its falls, Race Brook traverses through a wider valley touched by filtered sunlight and lacy evergreen boughs. The trail and meandering stream share the same course as they continue westward. Then the trail crosses the brook on a small bridge and remains on the southern bank until reaching Race Brook's marshy headwaters. Often flooded in spring, the poorly drained headwater valley can dry out in late summer and early autumn. Without the flowing water, an almost eerie silence fills the forest. Passing a campsite, this one a potent reminder of why overuse of the woods can be a problem, the nose urges a faster pace. After bouncing between hard bedrock and soft ground, the trail reaches the gap between Everett and Race mountains and dead-ends at the Appalachian Trail.

Heading right (north), the Appalachian Trail takes about three-quarters of a mile to reach Mount Everett's 2,602-foot summit. During this time the trail gains almost 700 feet, offering a challenging course up an exposed south-facing ridge. Sunny days can become hot and sweaty affairs. Usually straight and climbing, the lack of topographic variety is a reminder of just how much mountain there is to Mount Everett. With the sun's direct and constant daytime attention, the land is dry. Pitch pine, chestnut oak and blueberries thrive. Rocks along the trail scrape and slide like glass chips. In contrast, during a storm, the steep slopes and open trail bed funnel rainwater, and in spring almost any rainstorm can turn the terrain into a muddy and slippery watercourse.

Lichens grow in even the slightest depressions in the exposed bedrock, whereas the higher bumps are more resistant and don't provide good lichen habitat. The softer layers provide nutrients and shelter. The harder layers become microscale canyons. A mutualistic relationship between fungi and algae, lichens can thrive where few other organisms could survive. They are often the first organisms to grow in an area, helping transform rock to soil. Some animals eat lichen, but it is rarely a preferred meal.

The Everett schist is a metamorphic rock, the layer being one of the first thrust sheets pushed westward during the Taconic Orogeny. Among the rock's sparkling metamorphic materials are hints of muscovite and chlorite. Products of deep burial, the Taconics' rocks were sediments worn from older mountains. Cooked by the earth's heat and pressure, these shiny minerals were forced out of the restructured materials. On a larger scale, the original rock layers folded and faulted into irregular curves. Some of the rocks on Everett and throughout the Taconics are frozen records of these flows and bends.

The views from Everett's summit are mediocre. Until 2003, a decrepit fire tower stood atop the mountain. Change at this summit is no stranger, as even the name has changed; the peak was known as Mount Washington in the 1800s. Although the mountain offers fair views in most directions, none of them seem to grab the eye or spirit like Mount Everett does from so many surrounding peaks. Being higher than all its neighbors, Everett's summit seems to flatten the land and peaks around it. While the eye may be a bit disappointed, the palate is sure to celebrate in the summer; the blueberries and huckleberries are almost overwhelming. Even the local wildlife, including skunks and bear, enjoy Everett's summer bounty. After a few minutes at the summit, depending on the heat, the season and the appetite, it is time to move on to Mount Race's much more impressive vistas.

The hike back down Everett passes quickly, but can be tiresome on toes and knees. Mount Race's lower ridgeline provides a benchmark. The thicker northern hardwood forest once again denotes the gap. Soils are thicker and water is more plentiful as well. After a few level steps and passing the blue-marked trail and headwaters of Race Brook, the trail begins its ascent of Mount Race. Once crossing through a small forested wetland, the trail pulses its way up the mountain. Trillium and bunch-berry decorate the area in spring. Never hard, progress is steady. The forest grades into drier communities with oaks, pines and birches replacing a more diverse community downslope. Blueberries and mountain laurel line the trail. Tree heights fall on top the ridgeline, where a stunted pitch pine community crowds the mountain's rocky spine.

Although lacking Everett's final 230 feet of elevation, Mount Race, by far, provides the superior mountaintop experience. Arguably, the view from Mount Race is the finest vista in the Taconics, and words alone can only begin to introduce the awaiting beauty. From Race's open summit, spectacular landscapes unfold to the north, northwest and southeast. To the south the Litchfield Hills bounce up from the Housatonic and its family of valleys. To the west and northwest is Alander Mountain with the Catskills popping up along the western horizon. The most impressive scene, however, lies to the north with the glacially sculpted, regional highpoint of Mount Everett stealing the scene. A little south of the summit another inspiring view peers down the Housatonic Valley as it flows south toward Long Island Sound. The high cliff here accents the area's mountainous character.

The route back from Race merely retraces the previous journey; however, there are a number of circuit hikes that a second vehicle makes possible. Each adds its own special accents—additional waterfalls, steep valleys and additional viewpoints—and can even shorten the trip in some cases. With numerous waterfalls, two prominent peaks and a variety of awe-inspiring views, these two peaks are easily among the most fantastic of Taconic destinations. ⋏

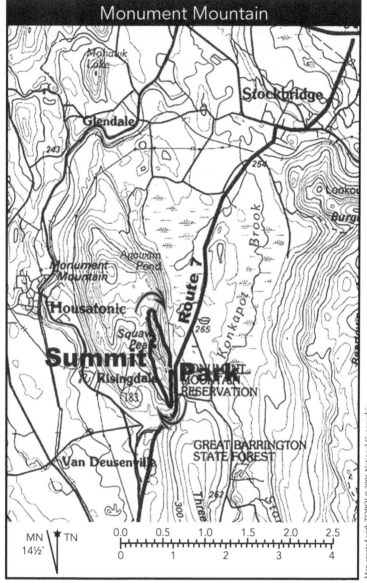

The Southern Taconics and Berkshires

102

Map created with TOPO! © 2006 National Geographic

MN 14½° TN

0.0   0.5   1.0   1.5   2.0   2.5
0   1   2   3   4

Monument Mountain

Highlight: View from Devil's Pulpit

Hike Length: 2.5-mile loop
Hike Difficulty: Easy to moderate
Starting Elevation: 939'
Highest Elevation: 1,642'

Directions:

US 7, 3 miles south of Junction with MA 102 (or 1.3 miles north of US 7 junction with MA 183). Parking is on west side of the road.

GPS

Parking:	42°14.59; 73°20.13
Squaw Peak:	42°14.83; 73°20.40

onument Mountain is well-named in many contexts, as its slopes are full of geological, industrial and cultural history. The trail begins along U.S. Route 7 from the large parking area facing a red pine forest. Red pine stands grow quickly, make great water filters and are a source of charcoal. Behind the pines' dark greens and reddish browns, a huge white cliff and its obligatory jumble of talus lifts toward Squaw Peak, which offers Monument Mountain's best views.

Monument Mountain is a multifaceted gem, its views being only one facet. The mountain's history, as well as its geology, shine brightly. The blocky, broken rock walls are a testament to the quartzite's hardness, among the toughest in the Berkshires or Taconics. On closer inspection, the lightly metamorphosed quartzite reveals its sedimentary origin, as the sands' cross bedding remains preserved within the rock structure.

Although Monument Mountain's peak is much lower than surrounding peaks, its resistant quartzite backbone is the reason any mountains at all remain in the wide Housatonic Valley. Other, less resistant, rock types and their resultant landforms were removed long ago.

From the parking area, a well-marked white trail, the Indian Monument Trail, begins a loop traversing Monument Mountain and Squaw Peak. Heading south (left) from the parking area, the first stretch of trail offers nothing more challenging than a few spreading roots and sharp stones. Once away from the red pines, a more random forest of oak, maple, hemlock, and birch grows from the rocky slopes. The light-colored rock is a lightly metamorphosed Cambrian quartzite, built from sands that were cemented and then altered under intense heat and pressure. Lifting and falling at a gentle pace, the trail slowly rises above U.S. Route 7, but remains near the thoroughfare. Sheltered by the nearby slopes, a comfortable hemlock forest creates a soft, shady and suddenly quiet spot.

Soon the trail reaches a sharp bend and turns north. The trail remains an easy walk while providing a good look into the middle levels of the neighboring forest. The trees are straight and tall, giving the forest the appearance of an older, storied wood. Tall white pines, declared the property of the British Crown in colonial times to provide ship masts, enhance the forest's openness and high canopy.

Then, the ascent begins. Old stone walls share silent stories about past farming on these slopes. In places the trail erodes deeply into the mountainside, a sign this path is old and improperly drained. For more than 150 years, Monument Mountain has been a destination for hikers, and to some people its cliffs and viewpoints were a pilgrimage. Artists and writers visited the mountain for inspiration and introspection. One notable visitor was Herman Melville, who may have received his inspiration for Moby Dick among these forests and viewpoints. Could the pale white rocks, with their massive, blocky forms, or some other local feature be the inspiration for his great white whale?

With the trail climbing steadily, a series of limited hemlock and pine-lined views to the southwest reveals Mount Everett and the more distant Catskills. Just as striking are the pleasant, rounded valleys that drain into the Green River. Gentle hills and meandering streams set upon fertile, nutrient-rich glacial soils make the landscape a mix of healthy forest and rich farmlands. Offering a few versions of this view, the first is the most expansive. Unlike the summit's dry and rocky slopes, the verdant surroundings here present a unique Monument Mountain viewshed.

Turning east (right), the Squaw Peak Trail heads to its namesake. Although Monument Mountain's true summit lies .9 miles to the northwest and is 90 feet higher, Squaw Peak has the impressive views. As the trail quickly becomes steeper, the route has more of a mountain character. After a short, tough climb, the trail reaches the rocky ridgeline holding the Devil's Pulpit and Squaw Peak. The pitch pine and birch forest thins and the sky shows through the sparse canopy. Light gray, lichen-frosted rocks poke through the thin soil and a rusty needle carpet. Dark and feathery hemlock foliage yields to oak, pine, chestnut, laurel and blueberry. Without the dense shade, the world brightens and on many days the air is noticeably drier.

Soaring rock walls foretell of additional climbing. The rocky islands arise like ship masts. In the same spirit, the best views from Monument Mountain peer out from their rocky crow's-nests. As a lingering comfort from the lower slopes, the trail retains a soft, needle-lined walking surface; however, it is now pitch pine, not hemlock, donating the spent needles. Rufous-sided towhees constantly sing the mountain's unofficial theme song.

Periglacial activity, in the form of almost daily freezing and thawing, has cracked, split and broken the mountain's cliff wall, generating deep and impressive talus slopes. Continuing to head north, the path ignores the first set of rock islands as it aspires to reach the well-named Devil's Pulpit. The blocky and massive light gray sandstones are now the land's dominant feature. In contrast with this dry environment, the gaps between the rock walls retain greater moisture and support forest stands more typical of the Northeast.

The trail looks toward the Devil's Pulpit, but with a bit of a climb remaining over difficult ground, the route veers west to provide a more reasonable approach from the north. Once reaching an unmarked junction, a side trail heads south, working its way to the Devil's Pulpit. Continuing to climb, the side trail quickly reaches the rocky perch that could easily be imagined as a summer home for the devil and his minions. A series of sharp, harsh rock pillars and cliffs fills the foreground. Pitch pine and mountain laurel are the dominant vegetation. Pines grow from the exposed surfaces, the lack of soil and nutrients supporting only specialized vegetation. In contrast with the surroundings, the heavenly view looks into the southern Taconics, anchored by 2,602-foot Mount Everett and 1,780-foot East Mountain. The glacial valleys, wide and smooth, contrast greatly with Monument Mountain's sharp angles and rocky cliffs.

The route retreats back to the Squaw Peak Trail and continues north to its namesake. The trail lifts an additional 150 feet to reach the open peak and continues at a moderate clip on the way to the 1,642-foot summit. The mountain's western face deflected the nearby road noise, but once atop the main ridge, the sounds of cars zipping along U.S. Route 7 return to the ear.

Atop the mountain, rounded quartzite boulders and broken rock fragments cap the mountain's angular form. Underfoot, rocks crunch like broken glass. Quartzite and sandstone bedrock breaks down into infertile sands, and the steep slopes prevent soil from accumulating. Almost crispy, a dry forest of oaks and pines covers the mountain, but just below the rocky spine the lighter, richer greens of mixed hardwoods cover the gentler slopes. On the mountain's lower slopes, more fertile glacial tills coat the ground and support a more diverse forest. Along the stream valleys and in more sheltered vales, darker hemlocks thrive. Cool, damp microenvironments along the water and the mountain's marginal fertility allow the hemlock to outcompete other species.

Not as high as many of the neighboring peaks, Monument Mountain felt the direct and uncontested force of the continental ice sheets. Situated in the middle of the wide Housatonic Valley, which held a massive tongue of flowing ice, much of Monument Mountain's mass cracked, broke and was carried away by the flowing ice tongue.

Set within the northeast view from Squaw Peak is a most curiously shaped wetland ... perhaps the inspiration for Melville's great white whale?

Without mountain neighbors to temper the icy blow, Monument Mountain was stripped, literally, to its mountain bones.

The glacially inspired view from Squaw Peak is outstanding, one of the Berkshires' finest. The mountain's position in the middle of the Housatonic Valley makes it a superior perch for views in all directions. The neighboring mountains hold blankets of trees and are ambassadors for recovering wilderness, while the valleys sprout structures born of man's labors spanning the last couple of centuries. Everything from schools to factories stands out in the valley, while summits from the neighboring Taconics and Berkshires, along with the more distant Catskills, outline the horizons. Incredible views of Beartown Mountain, East Mountain, Mount Everett and Bash Bish Mountain—all directly across the Housatonic Valley from the southern Taconics' high plateau—are displayed. To the north, Mount Greylock steals the show, enhanced by the low-lying forested valleys. Wetlands along the Housatonic River shimmer with green and silver. One nearby wetland even has the shape of Captain Ahab's famous nemesis. Even within the valley, the former site of glacial Lake Housatonic, some signs of unbroken nature remain.

The path down Squaw Peak drops quickly. Soon the rocky mountain islands fade into the thickening forest. A set of rough stairs eases the descent, but does not mask the sharp drop. The uneven steps make the overall slope easier, but with each step of varying length and height, flustered and confused cadences result. There are a few additional glimpses of the surrounding scenery, but never with the grandeur or attractiveness found on the summit. Once off the main ridge, the forest returns to the more fertile ground. Inscription rock is a notable trail stop. Here, part of the mountain's story is available for everyone—an appropriate message for this inviting mountain open to all.

The forest thickens, and a small stream and cascade escort the white-marked trail. Now called the Hickey Trail, it swings south to the parking area. A large and impressive hemlock forest lines the stream. The dark feathery evergreens take advantage of and enhance the cool conditions. They keep the forest floor in perpetual shadow, ensuring that few other plants take hold. Confusing side trails abound, almost beckoning wary hikers into the thick forest. Away from the stream grows a thick and lush northern hardwood forest. Then the trail works its way back to the parking area, ending the loop around Monument Mountain. ⚑

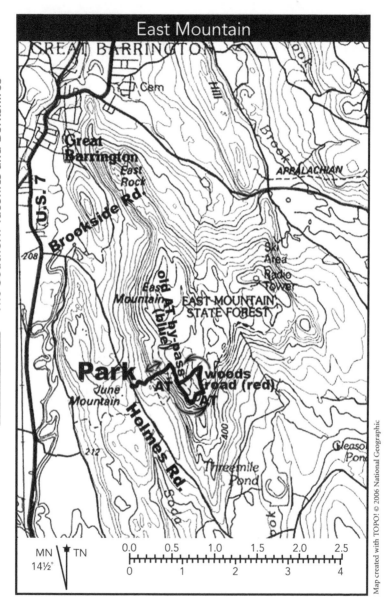

East Mountain

Highlight: View from first overlook

> **Hike Length:** 2.8 miles round trip
> **Hike Difficulty:** Easy to moderate
> **Starting Elevation:** 1,110'
> **Highest Elevation:** 1,780'

Directions:

US Route 7 south of Great Barrington to Brookside Rd. (east). Follow Brookside Rd. for .3 miles to where it becomes Brush Hill Rd. and then becomes Holmes Rd. for about 1.7 miles. Park on left (where Appalachian Trail crosses the road).

GPS

Parking:	42° 09.290; 73° 20.465
AT & Old Bypass Trail (first view):	42° 09.311; 73° 19.873
AT & Woodland Rd.:	42° 09.266; 73° 19.525
Jct. of Woodland Rd. & Old Bypass:	42° 09.441; 73° 19.631

Located just south of Great Barrington, East Mountain is an imposing mass bordering the Housatonic Valley. The mountain itself is made of resistant quartzite thrust over marbles during the Taconic Orogeny. Although it tops out at a modest 1,780 feet, the neighboring valley is 1,130 feet lower, enhancing the mountain's stature and the views. When driving along U.S. Route 7 and looking across the valley, a few rock ledges on East Mountain hint of its open views.

The wide Housatonic Valley provides access to East Mountain for people, and even for tornadoes! Mountains and tornadoes are rarely associated, but the Housatonic Valley in central and southern Berkshire County is a regional hot spot for tornado activity. On July 15, 1995, a severe thunderstorm raced across the Housatonic Valley south of Great Barrington, tearing across the Berkshire Fairgrounds before slamming into East Mountain. The tornado ripped up trees and buildings, leaving a swath of destruction still visible a decade later. A break in the forest cover, although healing, remains apparent.

A two-mile drive southeast on Brookside/Brush Hill Road from U.S. Route 7 intersects the Appalachian Trail (AT) as it descends June Mountain. June Mountain is the westernmost part of the Middlefield Thrust, an area moved via earthquake. The "mountain" is a long slender hill of Precambrian and Cambrian gneiss completely separated from any part of its parent material.

The route up East Mountain uses the AT. The path heads through a mixed forest dominated by white pines and red oaks. American beech, paper birch, yellow birch, sugar maple and red maple are other forest constituents. The red maples are easy to identify, as many display the specie's telltale "spider web" bark pattern. Small stands of hemlock round out this diverse forest, a product of the land's sheltered slopes, moderately fertile soils and moist environment. Many young trees populate the forest, the slender stems and limited ground cover creating an open feeling below the thick canopy. A few verdant ferns and colorful wildflowers decorate the ground. Poison ivy also lines the parking area and the trail's lower sections.

The trail climbs gently yet steadily. Remnants of field trees—white oaks in particular—spread conspicuously within the forest. Their squat forms and spreading branches are a liability now, but were the best forms to take when growing in these once open fields. As the trail climbs, it encounters the first of many rock outcrops. Here the land retains little water, and the vegetation changes. American chestnut, mountain laurel and northern red oak dominate these rocky slopes.

Although the precipitation is no less, fast-draining shallow soils generate a drier microenvironment.

The trail steepens as it hits the rock outcrops, but in places it levels off. Soon the mountain reveals the result of the climb from the valley. Here, mountain laurel, oak, and witch hazel dominate the forest, along with an increasing number of pine trees. Green schists, lightly metamorphosed sandstones and shales form the local bedrock—all products of deformation and metamorphosis. Deposited as sediments along long-vanished beaches and river deltas, these highly altered and erosion-resistant rocks now support Berkshire peaks.

Once bathed in the sounds of the Route 7 corridor, silence gathers as the trail divorces the road and valley. Moving up the rocky slopes, ice and wind begin to show their impact on the local trees. Twisted branches, broken limbs and stunted trunks become frequent. Tree heights begin to fall. A small view opens to the west that includes Race, Everett, and Bear mountains. After reaching the limited view, the trail undulates on a relatively level plain of about 1,600 to 1,700 feet. East Mountain's summit is wide and flat, more a plateau or eastern mesa than a classic mountain. Although there are many small changes in the local topography, the extensive mountaintop is generally level.

A small wooden bridge crosses a compact canyon. Within this gap a couple of loose boulders and large amounts of gravel fill the space. A glacial canyon, this curious landform resulted from either an Alpine glacier or an isolated corner of the retreating continental ice sheet. An ice-dammed lake provided, for a short time, a large volume of water. Once the ice melted or the dam broke, the water used this route—perhaps along a joint or other weakness in the bedrock—and carved this small canyon. The amount of water currently flowing through the intermittent stream and its canyon is far too limited to create this landform, even over thousands of years. This spot is a prime example of how the last ice age had a huge impact on the emerging landscape.

The trail begins another gentle rise. The mountaintop and its dry, sandy soils provide habitat for orchids and sassafras. Blueberry and its relatives become more prominent and make a welcome trailside snack in late summer. Bracken ferns are common, often growing in large colonies. The fern is distinctive because of its triangular orientation, and often has three major stems on each frond. It is a fire-adapted species, having deep rhizomes that survive light-to-moderate burns. Charcoal and ash make the soil more alkaline, allowing bracken ferns to reestablish quickly. Indians cooked and ate parts of the plant, but it can be harmful to livestock when consumed in large quantities. The fern produces an enzyme that destroys an animal's thiamine reserves.

Most of the rock here is schist. Some of the rocks show signs of heavy metamorphism. Wavy bands in the rocks represent plasticity during past heating and pressure events. The white rock is quartz, cooked out of the original rock chemistry. The trail skirts the mountain's rocky edge and hints at views, but offers nothing more than teases. A trail to the north (left), at one time a bad-weather bypass for the AT, forms the end of a loop over the mountaintop. The first views lie directly ahead. A few steps below the trail junction, an angled open ledge reveals a spectacular view.

Mount Everett and Race Mountain command much of the scene. These high peaks contrast with the U-shaped Housatonic Valley separating East Mountain from the rest of the view. Farther west rise the Catskills. In the valley below, development is a reminder of the balance man and nature struggle to maintain throughout the region. To the south are Connecticut's Litchfield Hills and the Riga Plateau.

After a bouncy trip along the cliff wall and an interruption by a small stream valley—another glacially enhanced landform—the trail reaches a second view. Although pitch pine joins the local flora, the view is less extensive. The trail then crosses, rather steeply, a larger valley. The cliff and outcrops look like mountain bones. The rock's resistant nature—some of the hardest in the Appalachians—keeps surfaces rough and raw. It also supports many of the weaker rock layers interspersed throughout these metamorphic layers.

Here, the forest has more moisture available throughout the growing season. One result is an increased contingent of black cherry. A few large, even impressive, American chestnut trees—a species nearly wiped out by chestnut blight—grow bold and large here. Although small compared to the size these majestic trees once attained, it is nice to find surviving remnants of this important species.

A third view reveals more of Connecticut to the south and east, but is mostly a repeat of the second view. The trail then eases as it heads north, reaching a fourth view. Here the scene opens up, looking downstream along the Housatonic Valley. Although dominated by lower hills, the landscape is vast. At this point, returning via the same route offers a recap of the four vistas.

If continuing on the AT, the trail climbs onto the mountain's wide summit before heading downhill. The forest recovers some of its stature, but the trees are young and skinny. The route then intersects a red-marked forest road and follows it west (left).

After .3 mile, the red-marked forest road intersects the blue-marked former AT bad-weather bypass. The junction is a bit tricky, poorly marked and comes in at an acute angle just south (hard left) and above the forest road. The old bypass trail, which is a bit rough in places, ascends the summit's plateau and moves directly through the terrain, in contrast to the AT, which traces the mountainside's varied landscape. The old bypass trail, after .3 mile, then rejoins the AT near the first viewpoint. One last peek of the views is available a few steps downhill from the trail junction. The hike concludes by retracing the AT south to the parking area. ⚲

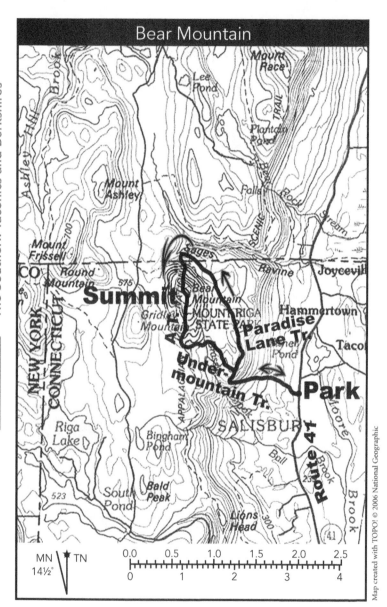

Map created with TOPO! © 2006 National Geographic

Bear Mountain

Highlights: Blueberries in July
View from the summit

Hike Length: 5.8 miles round trip
Hike Difficulty: Moderate
Starting Elevation: 740'
Highest Elevation: 2,316'

Directions:

CT Route 41 to 1.5 miles south of MA border (between Westmount Rd. and Foot Hills Rd.) Parking is on west side of the road.

GPS

Parking:	42°01.71; 73°27.73
Summit:	42°02.69; 73°27.30

A huge stone pyre tops Bear Mountain. Gray and imposing, the crude pyramid mimics a temple upon the mountain's 2,316-foot summit. Although this grandiose ornamentation marks Connecticut's highest mountain, this sanctified peak is not the state's highest point. Through a slight of geography, or perhaps a mean-spirited geographic joke, the state's highest point, which rises to 2,380 feet, lies just north of Bear Mountain on a southern shoulder of 2,453-foot Mount Frissell. Frissell attains its summit 500 feet farther north … in Massachusetts.

The most enjoyable approach to Bear Mountain follows the Undermountain Trail, which starts along Connecticut Route 41. A young forest boasts many slender, straight trees that line up like underage pickets. Well beyond the old field stage, the largest stems in this moderately aged forest reach about fifty feet. The forest composition reflects its pioneer status, fertile Taconic soils and the southern New England climate. A quick look into the forest reveals a collection of paper birch, northern red oak, white oak, sugar maple, red maple, shagbark hickory and hemlock. Time and random disturbance have huge roles to play in this forest's future, but for now this blend of northern hardwood and oak-hickory forest has more characteristics of the oak-hickory community.

The trail begins modestly, making a quick jump off the glacially enhanced valley floor. The valley once hosted Great Falls Lake, which spanned the northern Connecticut-Massachusetts border. Settling onto another flat shelf, the trail perches above the valley. Lining much of the trail, and giving the forest floor a lush appearance, is a thick fern understory. With reasonable soils and moisture, the forest also sports a healthy population of mushrooms and, in the sunny spots, white and purple asters. The area also has a rich bird population, and birdsong drowns out the less enchanting roadside noises. An intermittent stream runs alongside the trail for a little while, its watery influence supporting a population of dark-needled hemlock trees.

The area's land-use history is revealed in the strong presence of white ash, big-tooth aspen and white pine; these species are best at establishing themselves in old fields. Less than a century ago, this forest was used as farm or pasture, helping provide food for a mushrooming New York City population. Once the need for local food production was replaced by modern refrigeration and transportation, much of this land was no longer profitable farmland. As a result, much farmland in this and the neighboring valleys was abandoned to natural processes kept at bay for up to 250 years.

As the trail continues to move away from the valley, the route becomes steeper. Carving U-shaped valleys, the glaciers left wide, flat valley floors, but once heading up the mountainsides the steeper topography kicks in without much introduction. Depending on the land's orientation to the sun, the forest shows more characteristics of either the northern hardwood or oak-hickory associations. Slopes with southern and western exposure, which tend to be drier and warmer than east and south-facing slopes, often support the oak-hickory forest.

The maturing forest uses most of the available sunlight, so the forest floor is heavily shaded, keeping summer's heat at bay. Proud but sickly chestnut saplings, from the lingering root systems of this once-dominant tree species, are common. In this area it is easy to see a distinct three-layered structure to the forest—the canopy, an understory of more shade-tolerant trees such as maple, black birch and beech, and a prolific ground cover of ferns, shrubs and seedlings.

A sign announces the trail's entry onto Appalachian Trail (AT) lands. But the trail is steep, and labored breathing and rapid progress forestall stopping to think about the great trail and its history. Besides, crossing a line on the ground is not all that exciting compared to Bear Mountain's views and tasty treats.

The Taconic Mountains experienced today are a snapshot in geologic time. They have little resemblance to the 20,000-foot ancestral Taconics created hundreds of millions of years ago. Eaten by the elements over time, the great ranges have been ground to their roots, pushed, lifted and ground again. Rocks that were thousands of feet below the ground and hundred of miles closer to North America's eastern margin when the ancestral Taconic Mountains formed, now define part of our planet's rocky skin. Over time and through two more mountain-building collisions, the rocks upholding the Taconics and Berkshires melted, shifted, rose and came to the surface.

After a little more than a mile, the Undermountain Trail comes to a junction with the Paradise Lane Trail, which heads north (right) 2.1 miles to the AT. The junction is marked by signs and stairs. Ingeniously, both trails are marked in blue. Old stone walls and large outcrops typify the first stretches of the Paradise Lane Trail. Although never impressive, to the east are glimpses of the Housatonic Valley.

Climbing slightly, the Paradise Lane Trail lifts onto a dry, exposed ridge dominated by mountain laurel, blueberries and northern red oak. The vanquished American chestnut has a large residual population here as well. Windswept and open, sun and airflow combine to keep the area dry. Grass liberally sprouts from the ground, a sign of the area's pastoral past. The trail undulates about the ridge, but without much overall change in elevation. Not a difficult stretch, the gentle slopes leave more time for noting the flora and fauna. Birds dart in and out of the foliage. Rufous-sided towhee, American redstart, black-capped chickadees and downy woodpeckers are all common in this area.

The trail moves through a variety of environments. In one stretch the trail perches atop a rocky ridgeline where bear oak and pitch pine line the trail. The harsh, infertile conditions limit tree height to only 25 to 30 feet. The trees are widely spaced, and rocks displace soil as the main ground cover. In another impressive scene, the trail crosses a sea of walking ferns. A young forest rises above the ferns and will shade them out in time, depending on the frequency of disturbance. Soon after, the trail makes a sharp bend and follows the shady stream valley. Near the stream, hemlock is again the dominant tree. Tannins tint the water in tea tones as it steeps in the evergreen environment. To the west looms Bear Mountain's massif. Not yet ready for such a challenge, the trail turns away to take a less steep approach.

The trail skirts Bear Mountain along its northeastern flank. The trail is mostly level and heads though a mixed forest of oak, birch, pine and beech. Some areas are dry and rocky, while others collect water and form small wetlands. One of these nestles along Bear Mountain's northeast face, providing a comfortable and picturesque rest stop.

Finally, the Paradise Lane Trail intersects the AT a little more than 3.2 miles from the parking area. To the north, Sages Ravine slices the land and is one of the southern Taconics' more rugged and picturesque gaps. Heavily shaded and cool, hemlocks dominate the ravine's north-facing slopes. The trail crosses into Massachusetts just before reaching the AT. Once at the trail junction, Bear Mountain's massif rises to the south, with the AT leading the way. As the Paradise Lane Trail comes to an end, it engages in one last burst of psychological warfare, heading sharply downhill to meet the AT. Then, the AT immediately rises to regain the lost elevation as it returns to Connecticut.

To the north, the AT heads into Sages Ravine, a rugged, hard-to-access, steep and wild valley. Many cascades and an impressive stand of hemlock trees line this tight, isolated clove. Small waterfalls and cascades surge down the worn rocks and take the racing waters to the wider, gentler Housatonic. A trail, now abandoned, once headed up this steep valley. Still, the rugged, isolated cove is worth exploring in its own right, and although downhill from the trail junction, the short detour into the ravine compensates the eyes and spirit well. The cove's lower reaches can be accessed from Route 41.

Once on the AT, heading south to Bear Mountain, the trail heads though a beech gap. The silvery-gray trees dominate the forest. Beech gaps are found throughout the Appalachians. How they come to completely dominate some slopes remains somewhat of a mystery, but their ability to spread vegetatively allows them to build a strong network of clones. Unfortunately, this beech gap shows the effects of beech bark disease, and marred black trunks and fallen trees disturb the forest's integrity. Still, many of the trees remain standing, and a dark shade cools the ground. Combined with the north-facing slopes, the shaded ground can moderate an oppressive summer day into a much more pleasant experience.

After only a few steps through this peaceful forest, the trail blasts up Bear Mountain's north face. A set of chaotic rock steps helps pace the trail. Unfortunately, they tease tiring legs with a rhythm for a few paces, then stutter and lurch, breaking momentum and breathing patterns.

On this north face, sheltered from the sun's direct rays, the vegetation is thick, mainly oaks. The steep, shallow and rocky soils limit fertility, and the northern hardwoods can no longer compete. Even more chaotic is the local rock bedding. The metamorphic rocks glow white with bands of quartz set among darker schists. The wavering patterns of white, black and gray are hard to follow, jumbled and up-lifted in odd patterns. The harder surfaces create uneven, unpredictable traction surfaces, especially when wet.

The forest summit sustains mainly pioneer species since disturbance from both fire and ice is high. The mountain's upper slopes have even less vegetation and present a rocky landscape liberally sprouting oak, paper birch, pitch pine, blueberry, bunchberry and gray birch. Exposed to the sun, the slopes dry out and the vegetation thins, with most species well adjusted to the periodic fires that can scorch these dry mountain slopes. Blueberries abound on the summit and make a tasty treat in late summer—for people, birds and bears. A short time working the harvest will produce a large amount of sweet blueberries.

A large rock cairn, more of an informal monument than a mere trail marker, adorns Bear Mountain's summit. Built into a large platform, the massive pile is an obvious attempt to raise the summit of Connecticut's highest peak by lifting it the sixty-four feet necessary to make it the state's highest point. (Inconspicuously set on a shoulder of Mount Frissell about two miles to the northwest, the state's highest point is merely an innocuous spot on the slopes of Massachusetts' Mount Frissell.) Once atop the platform, there is a view to the north and west that takes in the Stockbridge Valley, Alander Mountain, Mount Race, and Mount Frissell, which rises about 250 feet higher than its visible neighbors.

Once over the summit and continuing south on the AT, the mountain provides a series of views to the south and west as the trail begins to work downhill. The Riga Plateau and generous eyefuls of surrounding Litchfield Hills fill the view. The hills roll on and on, stretching to the horizon. To the west rise Brace and South Brace Mountain, nearly equal in height to Bear Mountain. From these rocky viewpoints, the vista on a clear day will stretch west to include the Catskill Mountains.

Once off the pine- and blueberry-encrusted summit, a thicker, more diverse forest returns as water and soil become more plentiful. The views quickly disappear as taller oaks, birch and pine submerge the mountain in a sea of shade. Without much fanfare, the AT works steadily down the mountain, soon sprouting the Undermountain Trail to the east (left). Once on the Undermountain Trail, the forest community is more complex and lush. In spring an impressive display of purple trillium leaps from the forest floor like a tiny, yet intense, fireworks display. As it continues east, the trail crosses a few small streams, and the forest increases in diversity and height. Dark hemlock stands line the cool streams. After the Undermountain Trail intersects with the Paradise Lane Trail, the route retraces its steps to the parking area.

Bear Mountain is by far Connecticut's greatest mountain highlight. Although deprived of its title as Connecticut's highest point by a few dozen feet, its summit and vistas rate highest in the state. Its blend of forests, views, berries and exercise is sure to impress any explorer of the Taconics. ⊀

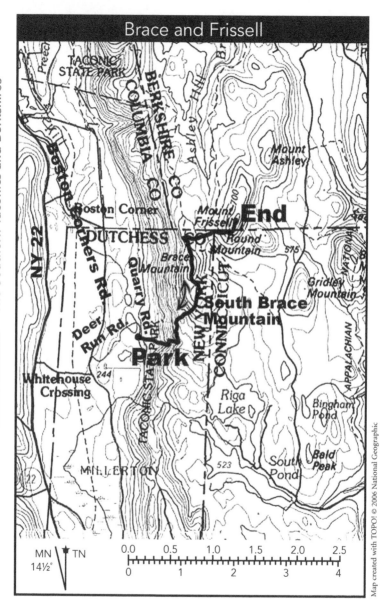

Brace and Frissell

Highlight: View from Brace Mountain

Hike Length: 6.6 miles round trip
Hike Difficulty: Moderate
Starting Elevation: 960'
Highest Elevation: 2,453'

Directions:

NY 22 to Boston Corners Rd. (east). Follow Boston Corners Road 2.5 miles (becomes Dutchess County Route 63) to Deer Run Rd. on left. Take Deer Run Rd. for about .4 miles to Quarry Rd. on left. After about .3 miles, parking area is on left.

GPS

Parking:	42°01.95; 73°30.28
South Brace Summit:	42°02.33; 73°29.44
Brace Summit:	42°02.66; 73°29.56
Frissell Summit:	42°03.07; 73°28.92

A lthough Dutchess County's landscape is dominated by the Taconics, only its most eastern ridgeline, extending along the border with Connecticut and Massachusetts, reaches Taconic Mountain status. The hills of Dutchess County top off as two higher prominences—Brace and South Brace mountains. To the east the mountains continue to grow, with Mount Frissell on the Massachusetts-Connecticut border lifting 150 feet higher than the Braces. Together the three mountains deliver a great 6.6-mile hike full of outstanding views, unique mountaintop environments and two important geographical locations.

The southern branch of the Taconic Crest Trail begins south of South Brace Mountain, rising through a steep ravine before reaching the Taconics' expansive ridgeline. The white-marked trail skirts an open field with a view north along the steep, high ridge. Rounded, smooth slopes delineate a mountain chain shaped and polished by glaciers. Both the mountain and neighboring valleys have the U-shaped contours distinctive of glacially eroded landscapes. A few exposed glossy gray ledges stand out among the green-clad mountains. The ridgeline shows few variances as it heads north and promises a tough climb. Blackberries line parts of the open fields, providing a treat for people and wildlife in late summer. Aspen and oak line the fields and sponsor the forest transition as the trail slips through the low trees into a larger forest.

Once in the neighboring forest, shade replaces sun and the air is often cooler and more moist. Bird calls fill the air, the blending of field and forest providing habitat for a number of species, including pileated woodpecker, bluebirds, tree swallows, red-eyed vireo and mourning dove. Sugar maple, American basswood, American beech, paper birch, yellow birch and northern red oak compose most of the forest canopy. Ferns and wildflowers add splashes of color to the understory.

Once establishing itself among the forest, the trail continues east toward the mountain ridge. The path winds between trees, becoming steeper as the route advances. Soon the sounds of a mountain stream filter through the forest and the trail heads into an isolated clove. Red trillium thrive on the moist, forested slopes. A damp coolness joins the air, as the stream acts as a natural air conditioner. Falling in line with the stream course, the water increases in volume and vigor. Across the stream, hemlock trees monopolize the cool, north-facing slope, while mixed hardwoods thrive on the sun-exposed south-facing slopes.

The sound of cascading water urges the trail upward as it parallels the stream. In an energetic contest, the trail and stream battle to see which is steepest. The stream wins, but only by a little as the rushing white water increases into a cascading sheet. The spreading waterfall is a series of drips, streams and plunges. Mosses and wildflowers coat most of the ground. Hemlocks provide a dark backdrop for the scene.

Rather than follow the waterfall, the trail veers north. Once out of the water's influence, the trail moves up and over an exposed rock wall. The open ground heats up rapidly in the sun and provides a great view west over the Taconic Hills, Hudson Valley and Catskill Mountains. Footing can be tricky among the tilted and bent rock strata, and finding good footholds competes for attention with the impressive viewshed. Along the rock face, the trail is more rock climbing than hiking trail. One of the few things growing on the rock is a lichen—rock tripe. Rock tripe looks like a brown potato chip, lighter on the top surface. Edible, this tough, leathery lichen has a mild mushroom flavor.

After climbing the rock wall, the trail and stream come together once again, but the landscape atop the ridge is much less lush than on the mountainside. The trail levels on an expansive tableland. Low oaks and mountain laurel dominate the open forest. Blueberries are a common ground cover. The stream has a small valley to call its own, and soon distances itself from the trail. Rocks continue to poke through the shallow soil, blending into a gray-green world that is neither lush nor barren. The occasional bloom of violet, blackberry, serviceberry or columbine adds gentle splashes of whiteness and color.

The temptation to stop at the first open viewpoint and take in the grand scene to the west is great. The Taconic rocks form hill after hill, like a giant set of stepping-stones, until they end at the Hudson Valley. On the valley's western flank rise the Catskills—an impressive mountain wall climbing to almost 4,000 feet. Open and exposed, the trail provides scores of these viewpoints, and they continue without pause until reaching Brace's summit. Stopping too quickly or for too long could mean taking in a scene eclipsed in beauty by the next viewpoint only a few steps farther along the trail. To the north, the wide gentle dome of South Brace Mountain shows that the Taconics offer more challenge than a quick steep jaunt up a ravine. Harder rocks support these taller peaks, the slightly metamorphosed shales much more resistant than the rocks to the west, including the higher Catskills.

Heading east, away from the ridge's steep edge, the trail leads straight for South Brace Mountain. Back to the southwest, the rugged Shawangunk ridgeline slices through the air. In a very real sense the Shawangunks are the geological child of the Taconics. As the Taconic Mountains eroded in the Silurian Period, about 390 million years ago, many of the sediments were carried away toward an inland sea. Deposited as river banks, mudflats and sandy beaches, this erosional cargo was buried deep beneath other sediments and slowly coalesced into new sedimentary shales and sandstones. As new mountain ranges formed along North America's east coast, first the Acadian and then the Appalachians, the Taconic sediments deformed and lifted to become new—recycled—mountains.

Ravens soar along the ridges, taking advantage of rising thermals along the valley's edge. The trail, however, heads deeper into the mountains, continuing to rise gently toward South Brace Mountain. Once in the shadow of the wide mountain, the forest thickens, with oak and birch continuing as its main components. Soon the trail approaches South Brace's upper foundation and must climb the waiting mountain. A steady incline awaits, the path providing an efficient route up the mountainside. Back to the south and west, the mountain—the southwesternmost point above 2,000 feet in the

Taconics—provides an overview of the Riga Plateau, the southern Taconics, the Hudson Valley, the Shawangunks and the Catskills. Lake Riga sits atop the plateau, the lake embedded into the tableland and surrounded by high hills and low mountains. Connecticut's Taconics are also called the Litchfield Hills, providing them more recognition as the Nutmeg State's highest terrain. Also apparent are some of the sparsely vegetated areas topping large sections of the rocky ridge. The bald, exposed areas are common in the Taconics and reminiscent of the Scottish Highlands. Occasionally a hint of bagpipes seems to slip by on the wind.

Open views along the Taconics' western front, including this one of Brace Mountain, are common.

The trees lose stature as the trail rises, the impact of winter wind and ice preventing the forest from reaching much higher. The wind is a often a companion along the Taconics, adding to the exposed environment. A little before cresting the summit, a trail junction cuts through the lowering vegetation. In a few more steps the oaks and birches cannot be considered anything greater than shrubs, as if they are not worthy of the mountaintop.

South Brace Mountain tops off at 2,304 feet and is carpeted in a generous blanket of berry plants and grasses. A small rock cairn sits on the summit, a feeble attempt to increase the mountain's elevation. South Brace opens on a great view to the south, including the stunning Lake Riga and on to the Hudson Highlands, Shawangunks and Catskills.

Leaving South Brace, the Taconic Crest Trail peers toward its next destination, Brace Mountain. Only seven feet higher than its southern namesake, Brace does not appear imposing or much of a challenge, but its open summit promises more great views. The mountain's most distinctive feature is its large rock cairn, which appears as a dark pyramid against the sky. As the trail dips between the mountains, the forest reasserts itself, with the oak and birch trees regaining some stature. No longer so exposed as on the highest ground, the wind often subsides, even as the sound of its passing rattles branches and leaves. Beyond Brace and farther east rises a more imposing mountain, Mount Frissell, which nestles in the middle of the southern Taconics.

The hike between sibling mountains is short, and the climb of Brace is easy compared to the climb up South Brace. South Brace fills the views to the south while ascending Brace Mountain. On approaching the summit, there is little doubt the open mountaintop will not disappoint, yet there is always something special about the view from the top. Awkward yet impressive, the mountain's rock cairn pinpoints the summit's location. Around the cairn, Brace's spectacular views unfold. It is hard to tell that South Brace, which fills the southern view, is any less of a mountain than Brace itself. In the southwest, the Catskills, Shawangunks and western Taconics sandwich the Hudson Valley. To the east and northeast, Bear Mountain and Mount Frissell give depth and definition to the Taconics' southern reaches. The trees remain stunted, but are larger than on the summit as the mountaintops provide shelter from some of winter's fiercest winds and ice. Still, the twisted trees cannot completely shade the ground, and grasses, berries and laurel grow thickly on the forest floor.

Cloud, shadow and sun play a vibrant game along the Taconic ridgelines. When it is cloudy, this area has a muted look, the bleak and desolate scenes typified by the Scottish Highlands. Often, fog dances with the mountaintop trees, leaping and plunging over the summits before losing form and substance in the valleys. The sun, however, paints a different picture. Colors become intense. Gray rocks sparkle, their biotite and mica stealing the scene. Quartz veins gleam in their brightest whites, like pearly mountain smiles. Reds and brown seem to jump from the landscape like a faded painting receiving a touch-up. Even the stoic oaks lose a bit of their pallor.

North of Brace Mountain, the trail makes an easy descent into a small gap. Wide and well-maintained, the trail rolls along as a comfortable, rocky path through a short, well-groomed forest. In the notch, replete with golden grasses and thick patches of oak and birch, a view opens to the west. The scene gives a great overview of the hike's past and future, revealing the gentler slopes of the Braces and the more mountain-like character of Mount Frissell. A trail junction marks the route to Mount Frissell, which soars into the sky well above the Braces. A trail sign provides the distance to some local landmarks, including Mount Frissell a mile away. The gap is a good place to observe how proportion and perspective work together to make the southern Taconics appear more impressive as a mountain range than their elevations suggest. Low surrounding valleys make the mountains appear high and foreboding. Erosion-resistant rock allows steep slopes to remain relatively stable. Close summits separated by deep gaps add to the perception of high peaks isolated by steep ravines. The unbroken curves shaping most of the local mountains bring an uninterrupted flow to the scene.

Leaving the Taconic Crest Trail to follow the red-marked Mount Frissell Trail, elevation falls rapidly as the trail heads into the gap between Brace and Frissell. A valley along Brace's southern flank makes this course the best crossing from Brace. Oak, mountain laurel and blueberry cover the sandy mountainside. Conspicuously, there are few pines. The area feels dry, the sandy soil unable to retain much moisture. The trail moves without difficulty through the gap, where an unmarked trail crosses the path. The trail then begins to work its way up Frissell's southwestern slopes. After only a few steps a granite marker appears, looking like an oddball tree. The post marks the tricorner of Connecticut, New York and Massachusetts. Placing an object on top of the marker places it in three states at once. Oddly, Connecticut is not noted on the marker, since at the time of the marker's placement, in 1898, the Nutmeg State was involved in a border dispute with New York. To help alleviate any confusion, the marker has been informally inscribed with "Conn." on the appropriate side. The forest, however, seems unconcerned with the geographic highlight as it uniformly blankets the surrounding terrain.

Without regard for the landscape, the Mount Frissell Trail heads up Frissell's flank while tracing the Connecticut-Massachusetts border. The steep trail appears as if a giant lawnmower hacked its way through the forest. The wide trail just runs along the mountainside, oblivious to everything except its glaringly straight bearing. The trail and the forest are not harmonious here, and make one appreciate the value of a well-thought-out trail through the mountains. The forest is oak, mountain laurel and blueberry—all fire-adjusted species. Pines are absent, the soils fertile enough to support a deciduous forest. Up toward the top of Frissell's shoulder, the open rock ledge reveals a view to the west, dominated by Brace Mountain, and to the south, the Riga Plateau. The trail continues its upward venue with most of the short vegetation unable to hide the surrounding landscape.

The next landmark is the highest point in Connecticut, boldly marked with ... a brass pin. The elevation at this innocuous point is 2,380 feet. The green, oxidized brass marker is merely a point on the shoulder of Mount Frissell, which continues to add another 270 feet of elevation as it lifts into Massachusetts. The landmark is understatement to the extreme. There is a small rock cairn, a sad attempt to lift the state slightly higher, but the effort is more a monument to futility. Beyond the lack of dignity, the spot is little more than another point along the trail. Coincidentally, there is a limited view to the south of Bear Mountain, which at 2,316 feet is Connecticut's highest summit.

As the trail winds around the next corner, it opens onto a nice view to the south including Berlin Mountain, Round Mountain and Lions Head. This vista also delineates the route used by the AT. West of these peaks is the Riga Plateau. A few steps farther along is a good view to the east, spreading from Mount Everett and Mount Race south to Bear Mountain.

The summit is a gentle dome covered in a mixed hardwood forest. Tree heights are lowered, but the forest is thick. A register adorns the lonely summit, providing a link to some of the other people hiking to this isolated mountain.

Unless more than one vehicle is available, the only viable return is to retrace the route used to reach Frissell. Along the ridgelines, the views to the west present an enjoyable visual show. Neither of the Braces are difficult ascents. Once among the sharp and tilted rocks lining the stream valley and waterfall, the route requires more attention, as the steep drop is only a step away. Once past the waterfall, the danger passes and only a steep grade remains to torture knees and joints for a few more minutes. The last few hundred feet review the gentle forests, open field and parking area. ⚲

4

Shorter Hikes:
Berkshire and Taconic
Waterfalls and Overlooks

In addition to the mountain hikes, the Taconics and the Berkshires hold an amazing variety of impressive waterfalls and overlooks. Most of them are readily accessible by a short walk and are not much of a hike by themselves. Still, anyone wishing to get to know the region would not want to miss these geological gems nestled among the valleys.

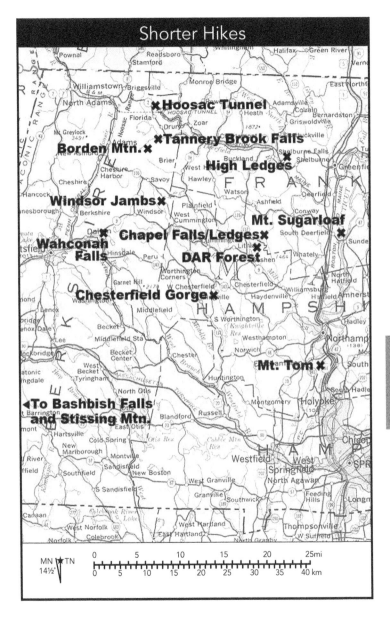

137

Wahconah Falls

Directions:

MA 9 to Wahconah Falls Rd. (on south side of road), which is 2.6 miles east of Dalton. Follow Wahconah Falls Rd. (becomes dirt) to park entrance on right.

GPS

Parking: 42°29.41; 73°07.03

Wahconah Falls is the namesake for Wahconah Falls State Park, a small park located just east of Dalton, Massachusetts, along State Route 9. A 0.1-mile walk along a gravel roadway leads from the parking area to a picnic area and the graceful waterfall. The fall spills in a wide fan-shaped cascade of about fifty feet. A calm plunge pool is studded with boulders—all victims of the fall's unrelenting erosional power. A couple of smaller cascades above Wahconah Falls add to the stream's charm. Within the small gorge containing the stream, hemlocks abound, their thick shade adding a year-round lushness.

Draining the Windsor Reservoir, the waters of Wahconah Falls Brook flow along Route 9 and through Dalton before joining the Housatonic River. Greenish schists and serpentine talcs form the bedrock supporting these falls. Iron-rich rocks, they formed as intrusions into North America's Grenville core before the Taconic Mountain-building event further deformed the region. Talcs are among nature's softest rocks; they are easily scratched by a fingernail. Mine shafts near the top of the falls brought these local talcs to the marketplace.

With a drinking-water reservoir as its source, Wahconah Falls Brook is a healthy stream and home to many salamanders. Just pick up a couple of rocks in or next to the stream and a salamander is likely to dart for safety. Salamanders breathe through their skin and secrete a sticky coating to improve the transfer of oxygen into their bloodstream. Handling salamanders removes this coating; thus, catching them with a net is a more humane choice. ⚹

Wahconah Falls is a great place to escape summer's heat.

Hoosac Tunnel

Directions:

Directions: MA 2 to Zoar Rd. (just east of Deerfield River bridge). Head north on Zoar Rd. for 3.3 miles (road crosses Deerfield River and continues as River Rd.) After bridge, continue for another 3.5 miles to parking area on right. River Road remains a scenic drive as it heads toward Readsboro, Vt.

GPS

Tunnel Parking:	42° 40.47; 72° 59.76

Although the Hoosac Tunnel is the focal point of this series of scenic stops, a number of pull-offs along River and Zoar roads offer short walks and scenic views that make the entire drive a pleasant journey, particularly in autumn. Among the highlights are the bridge at Tunnel Road and the many locations where the river approaches the road. Parking for the Hoosac Tunnel is available where the railroad crosses River Road. The tunnel lies to the west, with Cascade Brook following the track's northern edge. The stream leads about a quarter mile back to the Twin Cascades.

Sheltered from the sun by the Hoosac Range's northern flank, the area receives little direct light and offers a shady, moist environment. As a result, a lush forest dominated by hemlock, beech, birch and maple fills the ravine. Cascade Brook bounces playfully at the bottom of the water-carved V-shaped valley, sometimes dropping a few feet at a time before spilling into the Deerfield River.

Although known for its scenic beauty and autumn splendor, the Deerfield River's vigor and energy has led to the construction

The Hoosac Tunnel stretches for eight miles beneath the Hoosac Mountains, connecting the Deerfield Valley with North Adams.

of numerous dams along its seventy-three-mile course. Competing with recreational uses, water releases from the dams override most of the river's natural flows and dictate most of its water levels. When venturing anywhere near the river, it is important to remember that water levels can rise abruptly without warning at any time.

The Hoosac Tunnel is a major Berkshire landmark and national transportation icon. Here, at the tunnel's eastern portal, this five-mile passage begins the course that takes it 1,750 feet beneath the Hoosac Range. A major rail link between New England and the rest of the United States, the completion of this tunnel in 1878 was an important advance in transportation. The tunnel emerges from the Hoosac Range above North Adams, but the western entrance is not easily accessible.

With the tunnel's opening, transportation and industry brought a boom to the rural town of North Adams, which soon split from the more agricultural town of Adams. North Adams grew quickly, eclipsing its namesake. During the next 100 years, North Adams boomed and busted in transportation, textiles and then electronics. Now the small city's industrial and transportation economy is gone, but this picturesque town nestled between the Taconics, the Green Mountains and the Hoosac Range has a potential future in the arts and ecotourism. ⋏

Bash Bish Falls

Directions to lower parking area:

NY 344 toward MA border. Parking on south side of the road.

GPS

Parking:	42°07.03; 73°30.47
Falls:	42°06.93; 73°29.63

Sitting just west of the New York-Massachusetts border, this beautiful waterfall is accessed via a .75-mile trail from New York's Taconic State Park or a steep downhill walk from the upper Bash Bish parking area in Massachusetts. From the lower access to Bash Bish Falls, the trail follows Bash Bish Creek east, providing many accesses to the rock-studded water. The water often takes on the look of a light green crystal, while a myriad of reds, browns, silvers and greens fills the streambed. In more sheltered areas, hemlock trees dominate the forest, but yellow birch is more common overall. As a favored destination for generations, many paintings feature this picturesque fall. Asher B. Durand and John Kensett, among many others, painted the falls in the mid-1800s.

A few steeper sections lead up to the falls, whose flow dances with some impressive boulders. The volume of falling water is impressive, especially in spring. The site is a perfect canvas showcasing water, mountains and the ever-present power of gravity. Often crowded with people avoiding summer's heat, this popular spot is best visited off-season or during the early morning or late evening. Above the falls, the land becomes rugged, among the most inaccessible in the southern Taconics. Within its first mile of entering Massachusetts, the stream

Bash Bish Creek's steep journey out of Massachusetts ends with one last plunge over Bash Bish Falls.

gains almost 800 feet in elevation, and the gorge cut by the glaciers and Bash Bish Creek is more than 1,000 feet deep.

The upper parking area also is the starting point for a short rocky scrabble to an inspiring view into New York's Columbia and Dutchess counties. On the rock outcrop, schists and sparkling micas add to the perch's beauty. Roaring waters fill the clove with sound. The vista reveals the eastern Catskills across the Hudson Valley, but the perspective makes them look closer and higher than their true dimensions. Considering the ease of access, this view is among the most effort-effective sights in the Taconics. ⚲

Tannery Brook and Parker Brook Falls

Directions:

MA 116 to Center Rd. (just west of Savoy). Follow Center Rd. north for about 3 miles to junction with Adams Rd. Turn left on Adams Rd. After .2 miles, turn right onto New State Road. Head north on New State Rd. for 1.3 miles to Tannery Rd. Turn right on Tannery Rd. and follow 1.8 miles to parking area on right.

GPS

| Parking: | 42°37.30; 73°00.32 |
| Falls: | 42°37.44; 73°00.21 |

A short walk from the parking area deep within the Savoy State Forest leads through a hemlock forest to Tannery Brook Falls. The trail leads through a thick hemlock forest heavily carpeted in spent, rust-colored needles. Dark soils, scattered shrubbery and muted rocks complete the trailside accents. For most of its length, the route parallels Tannery Brook, heading down into a sharp valley at the junction with Parker Brook Falls. Steep and often slippery, the trail is not long enough to mount much of a challenge. With its uphill return, the trail offers a little more of a workout.

Tannery Brook Falls shows off a picturesque plunge pool at its base. A generous assortment of boulders allows for rock hopping and creates some excellent observation spots. Crayfish, salamanders and stoneflies are common residents beneath the stream's rocks. In summer this spot is one of the best for escaping the heat. ⚑

Tannery Brook Falls sits deep in the Berkshires, but is only a short hike.

Windsor Jambs

Directions:

MA 9 to W. Main St. in West Cummington. Follow for .1
miles to River Rd. Turn left on River Rd. and go 2.9 miles
to park entrance. Access to the falls is off the poorly
marked dirt roads to the east. Turn left on Windsor Bush
Rd. and continue for about a half mile (pass Windigo Rd.)
At the next intersection, turn right on Schoolhouse Rd.
Parking area is a couple of hundred feet up on the right.

GPS

Parking: 42°31.42; 72°59.51

Windsor Jambs is one of the coolest places in the
Berkshires—figuratively *and* literally. Ice persists
here, and many a warm spring day elsewhere trans-
lates into late shades of winter here. On the other
hand, the dog days of summer are little more than rumor among this
cool, dark, wet and shady corner of the Berkshires. Slicing into a slender granite canyon, this unique series of cascades is a relatively easy
walk from the parking area. Leading downhill along the gorge, the
trail works its way to the bottom of this white-water ridge. Promoting
safety, but destroying the Jambs' wild character, a chain-link fence separates visitors from the easy-to-access gorge. The ugly metallic fence
underscores how awkwardly people and nature can interact at times.
The fence also interrupts most of the area's photogenic features. Visu-
ally stunning in spots, the area is hard to fully experience as a whole.

Around the gorge, hemlocks dominate the forest, thriving
among the cool, damp landscape. Granite outcrops poke through

the shallow soils and form both walls. Without much sunlight or heat, moisture persists throughout the year, enhancing the local mushroom populations. ⋏

One of the coldest locales in the region, Windsor Jambs is lush and cool.

Mount Tom

Directions:

MA 141 to Mt. Tom park entrance (about 2 miles north of I-91 Exit 17). Follow main park road (Christopher Cross Rd.) to a 4-way intersection. Continue straight for .7 miles to parking area on right.

GPS

Parking:	42°16.31; 72°37.43
Goat Peak Tower:	42°16.19; 72°31.53

Mount Tom is the western branch of the Holyoke Range, the mountains separated by the Connecticut River. The entire Connecticut River Valley sits within an aborted rift valley that formed as the supercontinent Pangea pulled apart, 65 million years ago. As the land stretched and broke, magma came to the surface through oozing volcanoes and intrusive dikes that did not reach the surface. Geologically, this made the already complex rock structures throughout New England and the mid-Atlantic region even more convoluted. A number of these igneous structures are now at the surface. Along with Mount Tom and the Holyoke Range, they form many well-known present-day landscape features including East Rock and West Rock in Connecticut and the Palisades in New York.

Perched above the Connecticut Valley and sporting impressive vistas to the north and south, Mount Tom is a popular recreational destination. A beautiful mountain road traces Mount Tom's spine and offers easy access to the park's best viewpoints. A fire tower at Goat Peak offers the best viewpoint and is a quarter-mile walk from the parking area. The forest is second-growth mixed hardwoods, including healthy populations of northern red oak, American beech and various hickories. To the north, the lowlands along the Connecticut lend a pastoral flavor. The towers at the University of Massachusetts to the north, and the spires and buildings of Holyoke and Springfield, underscore this natural retreat's value. Sugarloaf Mountain and Mount Toby introduce the seemingly endless hills and low mountains to the north. To the south, rolling hills bump along the entire horizon. Perhaps most striking is the spine of Mount Tom and the Holyoke Range. ⋏

Mount Tom, part of the volcanic Holyoke Range, provides many commanding views of the Connecticut Valley.

Sugarloaf

Directions:

MA 116 to Sugarloaf St., which is .4 miles west of
Connecticut River bridge at Sunderland. Parking available
at bottom of hill and on the mountaintop.

GPS

Parking:	42°28.07; 72°35.70
Summit:	42°28.22; 72°35.51

S ugarloaf Mountain is a spectacular perch along the Connecticut River. Resistant sandstones uphold this rocky rise. Indian legends speak of this mountain as a giant beaver. South Sugarloaf, the lower peak, has a road to the top and a public-use area at its summit. A steep foot trail climbs the sharp southern face, and trails head down the western face, making an enjoyable loop. Combining the steep trail up the southern face with a downhill run creates one of the best compact workouts for casual runners or hikers. For those looking for less of a workout, the road up to the top offers easier access.

Once atop the mountain, a contemporary-styled viewing tower offers a wider view. To the south, the Connecticut River leads to the

Easy access to this perch above the Connecticut River makes Sugarloaf Mountain a popular destination.

Holyoke Range. Seeing how the river cut this igneous ridge in half is an impressive sight. To the east is 1,400-foot Mount Toby, its tower an obvious landmark. Almost directly below the summit, State Route 116 crosses the Connecticut River and heads into picturesque Sunderland. The view is among the most photographed in New England. North Sugarloaf is larger, offers a network of accesses and trails through a second-growth forest of birch, hickory, oak and maple, a wide variety of wildlife, and a couple of viewpoints of its own. ⋏

High Ledges/
Massaemett Mountain Fire Tower

Directions:

MA 2 to Little Mohawk Rd., 5.4 miles west of Greenfield Rotary/I-91. Head north on Little Mohawk Rd. for 1.4 miles. Then turn left on Patten Rd. and continue for .7 miles. **To Fire Tower:** Tower Rd. is straight ahead and leads .5 miles to a farm and the parking area for the Massaemett Tower. **To High Ledges:** The route to High Ledges bends to the right. Follow it for .7 miles, and then turn left toward High Ledges. Continue on the road for .5 miles where there are two parking areas.

GPS

High Ledges Parking:	42°37.04; 72°42.80
High Ledges:	42°37.17; 72°43.16
Tower Parking:	42°36.68; 72°42.50
Massaemett Tower:	42°36.41; 72°42.99

155

High Ledges offers a magnificent view of the Deerfield Valley, which happens to perfectly frame Mount Greylock, twenty-five miles away. The ledges are part of the High Ledges Wildlife Refuge and are also part of a larger sanctuary owned by the Massachusetts Audubon Society. The site's two highlights are the ledges themselves, which offer the compelling vista along the Deerfield River, and the impressive population of pink lady slippers that grow with almost reckless abandon. From the parking area, it is only a quarter-mile walk to the ledges. The refuge offers a few additional miles of hiking through a pleasant second-growth forest, visiting playful streams, healthy forests, comfortable valleys and an explosion of wildflowers.

Among the most prominent features above the Deerfield Valley in the Shelburne area is a curious circular tower topping Massaemett Mountain. Although the peak rises only 1,590 feet, the tower, looming above the famous Mohawk Trail, is a significant Berkshire landmark. A short, steep trail to the tower leads up from the Deerfield Valley, gaining 1,100 feet in less than a mile. A much easier trail of about the same length begins at a local maple farm off of Cooper Road. The access works its way along grass tracks and maturing forests to the main ridgeline and tower. Atop the medieval-looking stone tower is a metal observation box creating an ugly sheet metal crown for this architectural gem. Small openings at the top of the stone structure offer slices of the 360-degree view. The view stretches into Vermont and New Hampshire and highlights many of the region's highest peaks, including Mount Ascutney, Monadnock Mountain and Mount Wachusett. ⟡

One of the Berkshires' easternmost lookouts, High Ledges peers up the
Deerfield Valley with Mount Greylock in the distance.

Chapel Falls/Chapel Ledges

Directions:

The parking area for Chapel Falls/Chapel Ledges is located 6.5 miles north of Williamsburg, MA. Turn north in the center of town onto North Street, which becomes Ashfield/Williamsburg Road.

GPS

Parking: 42°28.97; 72°49.59

Nestled near Ashfield's border with Williamsburg, this short hike to a magnificent ledge with a sunny disposition and a nice view also includes a short walk to a series of three beautiful waterfalls. Owned and maintained by The Trustees, a nonprofit land conservation agency, this location is one of the best options for a short outing. A steep trail offers a quick workout before ending atop the small, Goshen quartzite highland. The view from the ledge includes the fire tower topping Moore Hill in the DAR State Forest, and a look south along the Branford Brook valley. The hill just south of the ledge is the divide between the Mill River, which flows south, and Deerfield River, which flows north. As a south-facing, somewhat sheltered viewing platform, this spot can be comfortable well into the fall and unbearably hot during summer's dog days. A sprinkling of pitch pine, white pine and birch grows along the cliffs, while a mix of hemlock, oak and hickory dominates the surrounding forest.

The falls offer no workout for the legs, but are an adventure for the eyes. Intimate, with its hemlock forest and series of cascades and falls, the photogenic site is a favorite of locals looking to escape summer heat and civilization. Together, the falls and ledges are one of the best easy-to-reach destinations in the eastern Berkshires. ⚊

Chapel Falls in Ashfield is among the easiest Berkshire waterfalls to reach.

Chesterfield Gorge

Directions:

MA 143 to Ireland St. (about 1.5 miles west of Chester-field). Head south on Ireland St. for .8 miles. Turn left onto River Rd. Parking area on left.

GPS

Parking: 42°23.65; 72°52.83

Chesterfield Gorge is a box canyon carved by the Westfield River. Well over 100 feet high, the steep Devonian-era gray schist walls hem in the river among the upturned strata. Once eroded into the rock, the river had an easier time removing the material along the rock's weaker area, and commenced in eroding a short, tight canyon. Picturesque, with green and white water, the site is great for a short walk. A dirt road parallels the river and works its way onto state land. The entire stretch of the river is among the best trout waters in Massachusetts. In colonial times an old stage road passed through the area, crossing the river near the gorge on a high bridge. The road ceased operations in 1875. ⸙

The canyon holding the Westfield River is an impressive geological formation.

DAR Forest and Tower

Directions:

Front entrance:

MA 112 to Park entrance (.7 miles north of junction
with MA 9). Turn right on Moore Hill Rd. (park entrance).
Parking area on left.

Rear entrance:

Williamsburg Rd. (2.8 miles south of junction with MA
116) to Ludwig Rd. Head west on Ludwig Rd. Enter park
after .7 miles. Follow Moore Hill Rd. for .5 miles to Tower
Rd. Turn left and follow .4 miles.

GPS

Main parking:	42°27.40; 72°97.46
Rear entrance:	42°28.17; 72°46.64
Tower:	42°27.88; 72°27.01

From its main entrance (fee charged), this park offers a moderately challenging hiking loop as the best chance to access the park's eighty-foot fire tower atop Moore Hill. The hike crosses a number of ridges as it rises to meet the fire tower. An alternate route along the park's main road makes this hike even shorter, but less interesting.

Still, a greater shortcut remains. The west side of the park is accessible from South Ashfield Road, and when the gate there is open, there is direct driving access right up to the fire tower. Even when the gate is closed, it is only a .7-mile walk to the top. The fantastic 360-degree view from the tower, which encompasses mountain peaks from Wachusett to Greylock, requires more elevation gain than the walk from the gate.

In winter, Lower Highland Lake freezes over and is a favorite destination for cross-country skiing, hockey, snowshoeing and ice fishing. The experience of walking out into the middle of the lake and safely standing on a huge sheet of ice makes the DAR forest a great winter destination. ⚡

Borden Mountain

Directions:

MA 116 to Center Rd. (just west of Savoy). Follow Center
Rd. north for about 3 miles to junction with Adams Rd.
Turn right and go about .5 miles until reaching a gated
pull-off.

GPS

Parking:	42°36.39; 73°01.87
Tower:	42°36.06; 73°01.65

A southern member of the Hoosac Range, Borden Mountain has a cleared summit, an intact fire tower and a host of radio equipment. The tower is currently not open to the public. The half-mile hike up this mountain is a moderate walk up a dirt road. A second-growth forest, mainly hardwoods, covers the mountain. Views along the road and from the summit focus on the north, revealing the Hoosac Range and stretching into Vermont. ⚮

The Mount Greylock massif, including Saddle Ball Mountain, stands out from the fire tower atop Borden Mountain.

Stissing Mountain

Directions:

From Pine Plains head south on NY 82 for .4 miles. Take
right on Lake Rd. and follow for 1.6 miles. Parking on
right; trailhead on left.

GPS

Parking:	41°96.99; 73°68.21
Summit:	41°96.41; 73°68.75

Although the Taconic Mountains dominate Dutchess and
Columbia counties in New York, it is the wide and fertile
limestone valleys that characterize much of the landscape.
Slabs of Taconic strata lift hills and create a complex topography. Some of the hills are open and present various views of
the Catskills to the west and the Taconic Mountains to the east and
northeast; however, only a few perches in these bumpy foothills man-
age to graduate from pleasant and pastoral to awe-inspiring. Stissing
Mountain is the best example of such grandeur, its glacially scoured
eastern face rising almost 1,000 feet above Thompson Pond, the headwaters of Wappinger Creek.

Stissing Mountain offers a short, but steep, half-mile climb up 700
feet of its northwestern face. The trail begins along Lake Road a couple
of miles west of Pine Plains. The steep trail offers no warm-up, and
the route is well-marked along its first stretch. Upon reaching a less
steep woods road, however, the trail signs cease and the rocky terrain
challenges ankles. A vigorous young forest of mixed hardwoods covers
the slopes. Oak, birch, maple and beech are all common. White pines
emerge from the forest canopy at irregular intervals. Soon the trail

branches, with the right branch offering a slightly longer (by .2 miles) and less steep route to the summit. The left branch is all business, but does offer an ample opportunity to pick blueberries in season.

The view from the ninety-foot steel tower erected near the 1,403-foot summit is the mountain version of Times Square. Mount Everett and Mount Greylock crown the southern Taconics, while the eastern half of the Catskills lines the western horizon. To the southwest the Shawangunks rise like a wide highland, belying their slender mountain lines. The Hudson Highlands, eroded remnants of ancient North America, rise to the south. Connecticut's Litchfield Hills round out the mountain panorama. Directly below the mountain spread wetlands, fields, forests and villages. Greens and golds coordinate the scene. And, with just a little imagination, Stissing Pond's outline reveals a flying eagle, a giant shadow of what can sometimes soar above the tower. Although it is not a huge mountain or a long hike, Stissing Mountain's view is among the region's most impressive. ⋏

Notable Taconic and Berkshire Elevations

Mount Equinox	3,848'	Mount Frissell	2,453'
Dorset Mountain	3,770'	Mount Race	2,372'
Mount Greylock	3,491'	Mount Anthony	2,342'
Mother Myrrick Mountain	3,352'	Bear Mountain	2,316'
		Brace Mountain	2,311'
Little Equinox	3,310'	South Brace Mountain	2,304'
Saddle Ball Mountain	3,238'	Alander Mountain	2,235'
Mount Aeolus	3,208'	Lenox Mountain	2,150'
Mount Fitch	3,100'	Yokun Seat	2,135'
Mount Williams	2,956'	Bash Bish Mountain	1,890'
Crum Hill	2,841'	East Mountain	1,780'
Berlin Mountain	2,818'	Monument Mountain	1,735'
Spruce Mountain	2,730'	Squaw Peak	1,642'
Mount Everett	2,602'	Massaemett Mountain	1,590'
Mount Raimer	2,575'	Stissing Mountain	1,403'
Spruce Hill	2,566'	Mount Tom	1,202'
White Rocks	2,542'	South Sugarloaf Mountain	652'
Borden Mountain	2,510'		

SELECTED BIBLIOGRAPHY

Writing a book about exploring the Taconics and Berkshires required many kinds of adventuring. The physical work is only part of the adventure; much of the quest was conducted in research before and after taking the actual hikes themselves. While the land itself shares many stories, many more are found in the works of others. A wide selection of titles has added to the content in *Berkshire & Taconic Trails*.

Time has brought many changes to the region. Geology texts like *Roadside Geology of Massachusetts* by James W. Skekan (2001), *Roadside Geology of New York* by Bradford B. Van Diver (1985), and *Roadside Geology of Vermont and New Hampshire* by Bradford B. Van Diver (1987), all published by Mountain Press Publishing Company, Missoula, Montana, reveal how the region's rocks and landforms evolved. A great overview of the geology of the Northeast, including the Taconics and Berkshires, is provided in *Written in Stone: A Geological History of the Northeastern United States* by Chet Raymo and Maureen E. Raymo (3rd edition, 2007, Black Dome Press, Hensonville, New York). For a detailed examination of the last ice sheet's influence on the area, look for *The Wisconsin Stage of the First Geological District, Eastern New York*, edited by Donald H. Caldwell (1968, New York State Museum Bulletin Number 455, Albany, New York). Another detailed look at the region's geology is available in *The Rise and Fall of the Taconic Mountains: A Geological History of Eastern New York* by Donald W. Fisher (2006, Black Dome Press, Hensonville, New York).

The forest, too, has many hidden stories to tell. *Forested Landscape* by Tom Wessels (1999, The Countryman Press, Woodstock, Vermont) is an excellent guide to discovering these stories. There are many natural guides that cover the area, but one, the *Bird Finding Guide to Western Massachusetts* (Oritz et al., 2003, University of Massachusetts Extension, Amherst, Massachusetts) stands out as an excellent guide to the Taconics and the Berkshires.

Some of the Taconics' highest points have been the focus of publications of their own. *Mount Equinox Past & Present* edited by Susan Grant (1994, WIM Publishing, Middletown, Rhode Island) provides a guide and history to the range's highest peak, while *Most Excellent Majesty* by Deborah E. Burns and Lauren R. Stevens (1988, The Studley Press, Dalton, Massachusetts) focuses on Mt. Greylock, the highest point in Massachusetts.

The Berkshires have been a seat of American culture for more than 150 years. Changes to the landscape and the ways people have viewed and interacted with the natural world have been the topic of many books. Mt. Tom and the Holyoke Range is the subject of *Changing Prospects* edited by Marianne Doezema (2002, Cornell University Press, Ithaca, New York). *The Berkshire Hills* (a WPA Guide reprint, 1987, First University Press, Lillington, North Carolina) looks at the region through a Depression-era lens. *Taconic Trails* by Edward Heald (1929, J.B. Lyon Company, Albany, New York) explores the western Taconics in the 1920s. *A Berkshire Sourcebook* by William Carney (1976, The Junior League of Berkshire County, Inc. Pittsfield, Massachusetts) provides a more modern view of life in the region, but as the decades pass, it too is beginning to fade from first-hand experience and into history.

Any examination of the Berkshires' culture cannot be complete without a discussion on the art of the nineteenth-century Hudson River School of landscape painting. Many views of the region adorn canvases from that era. *A Return to Acadia* by Maureen Johnson Hickey and William T Oedel (1990, The Studley Press, Dalton, Massachusetts) includes many images from scenes along the hikes featured in this book. *Art and the River* edited by Nancy Goldberger and Andrea Scott (Sheffield Art League, North Adams, Massachusetts) shares the imagery of the Housatonic River Valley and the surrounding mountains, connecting the artistic grandeur and admiration of previous generations with the more intimate explorations of today's outdoor enthusiast.

ABOUT THE AUTHOR

Photograph by Dan Stotts

Edward Henry grew up just outside of Woodstock in the Catskill Mountains. He has been exploring and writing about the Appalachian Mountains and surrounding regions for the past twenty-five years.

Besides his adventures in the Taconic, Berkshire, Catskill, and Shawangunk mountains, Henry has worked for the National Park Service and as a park ranger in the Shenandoah and Great Smoky Mountains National Parks. He now works for the U.S. Fish and Wildlife Service and is the Refuge Manager for the Wallkill River and Shawangunk Grasslands National Wildlife Refuges.

Henry is the author of three other books: *Catskill Trails: A Ranger's Guide to the High Peaks, Book I, The Northern Catskills; Catskill Trails: A Ranger's Guide to the High Peaks, Book II, The Central Catskills* (Black Dome Press: 2000) and *Gunks Trails: A Ranger's Guide to the Shawangunk Mountains* (Black Dome Press, 2003), plus numerous magazine articles. He is also an active speaker on environmental issues and natural history, co-hosts a community access television show, is an active storm chaser, a part owner of The Reservoir Inn in West Hurley, New York, and is a freelance landscape photographer with numerous awards and many photos in publication.

Henry has a master's degree in forest ecology from SUNY's College of Environmental Science and Forestry in Syracuse, New York. He presently lives in Wurtsboro, New York.

INDEX

W

Y